the
inbetweeners
moving on

the
inbetweeners
moving on

MATTHEW RICHARDSON
AND MIKE DODGSON

JOHN BLAKE

Published by John Blake Publishing Ltd,
3 Bramber Court, 2 Bramber Road,
London W14 9PB, England

www.johnblakepublishing.co.uk

www.facebook.com/Johnblakepub
twitter.com/johnblakepub

This edition published in 2014

ISBN: 978 1 78219 985 4

British Library Cataloguing-in-Publication Data:

A catalogue record for this book is available from the British Library.

Design by www.envydesign.co.uk

Printed and bound in Great Britain by CPI Group (UK) Ltd

1 3 5 7 9 10 8 6 4 2

Papers used by John Blake Publishing are natural, recyclable products made from
wood grown in sustainable forests. The manufacturing processes conform to the
environmental regulations of the country of origin.

Every attempt has been made to contact the relevant copyright-holders, but some
were unobtainable. We would be grateful if the appropriate people could contact us.

Matthew: Dad, here's another one for the bog :)
Mum, Si & Liv, thanks for putting up with me!
And Jade, the first book you'll have read in years. Enjoy x

Mike: For Nikki, thank you for the past 2 years,
I owe you some time back!

CONTENTS

INTRODUCTION

Since 2008 *The Inbetweeners* has taken us on a comedy journey about growing up and getting laid (sort of!). Throughout the years the lads have bunked off school to get drunk, worn a tramp's shoes in a London club, torn up the town at caravan club and lived the life on the ultimate lads' holiday in Malia! We've heard new levels of stupidity from Neil and been introduced to all kinds of phrases new to the English language, such as 'bumder' and 'OA-Peado!' Now, with what surely has to be one last hurrah, the *Inbetweeners* have taken themselves to the travellers' trail in Australia to take in a bit of culture and, of course, to find some 'clunge'!

It's not only the characters who are flourishing; most of the actors and actresses have started to bloom with fantastic careers on the back of the success of *The Inbetweeners*. This book brings us up to date with what the actors and production team have been doing since the series. There's info on the sitcom *Chickens*, which was written by Simon Bird and Joe Thomas along with their university mate Jonny Sweet; *Cuckoo*, the comedy starring the legend that is Mr Gilbert, aka Greg Davies; and *Drifters*, dubbed the female version of the show and starring girls from the movie. You can also find out which *Inbetweeners* star featured in hit movies alongside Hugh Jackman and Colin Firth in *Les Misérables* and *The King's Speech*.

So where are we up to in the lives of our favourite pupils of Rudge Park Comprehensive School? We last saw Will, Simon, Jay and Neil landing back in the UK after what can only be described as a disaster of a lads' holiday in Malia. The 'coming of age' holiday that all teenage lads see as the 'holy grail' came about through Simon getting dumped by Carli. However, it wasn't quite the 'sun, sea and sex' fest the lads (especially Jay) had planned; the four got into all sorts of hilarious situations (who could forget the famous dancing scene in the club?) that left fans like us wanting more!

The Inbetweeners: Moving On reminisces over the good times and basks in all the funniest moments since the show started. It takes you through the best bits we've seen so far from the show and first movie and gives you the scoop on all of the gossip to get you ready for the eagerly anticipated second movie.

You can swot up on all of your *Inbetweeners* knowledge with a full list of every character and actor we've seen so far, loads of funny quotes and plenty of interesting facts. What's more, check out what the main actors Simon Bird, Joe Thomas, James Buckley and Blake Harrison are doing now: who's married with kids, who ended up in a river on a stag party and who is dating a soap actress.

THE INBETWEENERS

As avid fans of *The Inbetweeners* themselves, and writers of *The Inbetweeners A–Z*, Matthew Richardson and Mike Dodgson are the perfect people to take you through to the next stage of one of Britain's funniest and most successful comedy shows.

Read this book from start to finish or dip in and out of it – it's up to you!

CHAPTER ONE

THE LEGACY

SERIES 1 – WHERE IT ALL STARTED

When Polly Mckenzie can no longer afford the expensive fees for her son Will's private school, she decides it's best to enrol him in a local comprehensive, Rudge Park. For middle-class Will, who has been used to the finer things in life, this is something of a culture shock. And to his surprise, the other kids don't take too well to his blazer, briefcase and 'MY NAME IS WILL STOP ME and say HELLO' badge. His first day starts with a picture of him taking a dump in the school toilets getting posted on noticeboards around the building.

In the first episode, Simon is forced by sadistic Head of Sixth Form, Mr Gilbert, to take Will under his wing. Mates with 'filthy bullshitter' Jay Cartwright, and not-so-sharp Neil Sutherland, the three certainly aren't the coolest kids in school but even for them Will is a bit of a geek. Still, after a bit of persuasion and a lot of lingering, they finally accept that Will is part of their group and in the first series of the show we see them get into some hilarious situations.

'Briefcase Mong' Will starts his schooldays as he means to go on. By pissing off his fellow students, including Rudge Park bully Mark Donovan. At the ritual underage boozing session at the Black Horse/Bull, when Will doesn't get served for being a minor, he decides to have a rant at the barman, explaining that everyone in there is his age too. Funnily enough, this doesn't go down too well with the others and Will certs himself as the biggest pain in the arse at the school.

In the second episode Will does make a bit of an attempt to show the others that he isn't the geek they think he is by eventually agreeing to bunk off school with them for a day of girls, booze and more girls.

So, out to impress, Will raids Simon's Dad's wardrobe and, 'dressed like a Hassidic Jew', heads to the off-licence to stock up. The plan actually works to an extent and he manages to score some booze, although the others aren't too impressed with his choices: party snacks, gin and whisky liqueur!?! Still, they decide to make the most of it and head to Neil's house to get the party started.

Unfortunately for the boys, the day doesn't go quite as planned and, after realising there are no girls to party with because they're all back at school, the lads get smashed playing drinking games, Will ends up hurling a load of abuse at Neil's dad ('Oh, you'd like my lip, wouldn't you? Right round your bell-end...you BUMDER!') and Simon ends up spewing all over Carli D'Amato's kid brother after making a fool out of himself by spray-painting his love for her on her parents' front driveway.

Things start to look up for the boys in the next episode, when

Simon, with a lot of help from a very forward female examiner, manages to pass his driving test. The world is now their oyster; they can go where they want, when they want, without the involvement of interfering parents. Festivals, holidays, road trips… well, not quite. On Will's recommendation and with some persuasion from Neil ('Sometimes on the rides their boobs pop out. You only get a split second of tit as they're going at about seventy miles per hour – still good though!'), they decide to take a trip to Thorpe Park.

Hardly the most adventurous option they could have taken but still, it's a trip out for the lads on the open road, where they're not bound by the rules of teachers or parents.

This turns into one of the classic episodes in the show and often a favourite with its fans. After a very cautious drive in the 'shit mobile' that involves getting caught up in a funeral procession, the gang make it to the park, where Neil ends up naked, Will ends up insulting a group of disabled kids and Simon ends up with one less door on his already shit car. The perfect day out then!

By now Will has managed to create a pretty bad reputation for himself through his uncool antics but, despite this, in the fourth episode of the first series, 'Will Gets a Girlfriend', the geek manages to score an invite to a houseparty. It's hardly the social event of the year but, after pissing off the entire Sixth Form in his first week, we reckon he's done well! After a bit of a slow start, to everyone's surprise, cool-kid Charlotte Hinchcliffe turns up and even more of a surprise is that she takes a liking to Will (despite Jay's attempts at wooing her with his Crazy Frog impression).

After a few intellectual ponderings in the kitchen, Will and

Charlotte head upstairs for some heavy petting, with Will even avoiding a beating from Donovan (Charlotte's ex, who catches the pair together). The new boy's luck seems to have turned a corner and the teens arrange to meet up again. Will knows this could be the moment he's been waiting for; his chance to lose his virginity... but worried about his complete lack of experience in comparison with Charlotte, who claims to have already had 11 lovers, Will decides to bend the truth a little when talking to her about his own sexual adventures. The Inbetweener tells the much more experienced sixth-former that he lost his virginity at just 13! It doesn't take long after they meet up again for Charlotte to realise, however, that he isn't as experienced as he's made out:

'Will, stop. Don't move your whole body, just your hips, you know... forget it, you haven't done this before, have you? I think the moment's gone, to be honest.'

And when Will asks her if he's now lost his virginity, she tells him he shouldn't be counting that one. Gutted.

So with that epic failure, another episode comes to a close. Next on the agenda for *The Inbetweeners* is a trip to the 'Caravan Club' at Camber Sands. Throughout the series Jay has been spouting off to the others about how this place is practically an orgy, telling them, 'First rule of Caravan Club is that everyone gets some.' It hardly looks like the sex-fest they've been promised as they arrive but, after bumping into a couple of girls, the lads remain fairly hopeful that Jay's usual bullshit isn't involved in his caravan stories.

So the optimistic foursome head off to the 'main event' at the club, a shitty party in a shitty hall on the shitty campsite. It would be an understatement to describe the night as an utter disaster.

Jay doesn't pull (for a change), Will gets his shoes robbed by a group of pre-teens and Simon almost ends up on a sex-predator list when he thinks he's 'in there' with Becky, the girl he met earlier, and pulls his pants down to his ankles outside the party! Of course, he wasn't in there and this is just a bit of a shock for the girl, who screams the place down, leaving the lads to head home the following day with their hopes and dreams of sex dashed again (besides Neil, who reveals that he managed a bit in the back of Si's car!).

Things do get better for Inbetweener Will in the final episode of the first series, 'Xmas Party'. Will finds himself in his element as the elected chairman of the Christmas-prom committee (being the only one to apply) and, with a bit of help from the others, organises a great event. Highlights of the prom night include Neil trying it on with Biology teacher Miss Timms while wearing a 1970s-inspired disco suit, Simon failing to win Carli over again and the Rudge Park sixth-formers sticking up for Will when bully Donovan prepares to give him a beating.

SERIES 2 – OUT AND ABOUT

In the second series of the show we see the lads venture beyond the walls of Rudge Park Comp on several occasions, getting themselves into countless awkward and hilarious situations, of course.

The series kicks off at the start of a new term at the lads' school and the boys have decided to sign themselves up for the annual Geography and Sociology fieldtrip to Swanage – this includes Neil, who doesn't even take either of the subjects.

They each have different agendas for the trip. Will is keen to explore the surrounding area and plans to take a scenic row on a boat down the canal; Jay is on the hunt for a legendary seaside MILF who he's heard chooses one schoolboy each year to show the ways of the world; Simon wants to impress new-girl Lauren, much to Will's annoyance; and Neil is looking forward to consuming the vodka he's received as a 'gift' from rumoured-paedophile teacher, Mr Kennedy, who personally invited him on the trip!

As you'd expect from the gang, the school outing doesn't quite go as planned. Jay doesn't find the MILF and instead ends up asking an old woman if she'll 'lick his Cornetto'; Neil's vodka is nicked by bully Donovan and he's forced to take a swim with Mr Kennedy in a pair of Speedos the teacher has supplied; and Will gets to take his boat trip but it ends with Simon naked with a sock on his penis and a dead fish – no chance of any girls for any of the lads.

In the next episode it's another school-related outing for the lads. This time though it's the dreaded work experience! Most teenagers see this as a couple of weeks of graft that they could do without but, as we've learned by now, Will isn't like most teenagers. Instead, he actually can't wait to sink his teeth into some real-life work, seeing his work-experience placement as a great chance to boost his university application with a week as a journalist planned at a local newspaper office.

The problem for Will though is that, through some sort of clerical error (we get the sneaky suspicion it's Will-hater and Head of Sixth Form Gilbert's doing), he ends up having his placement swapped with fellow Inbetweener Neil, whose planned work experience is in a car mechanics' garage. Neil isn't too fussed and just goes with the flow but Will is outraged at this injustice. His plans have been completely messed up and he feels he's got too much going for him to spend the week at a greasy garage. However, unsympathetic Gilbert decides to teach the 'job-snob' a lesson and tells him to get on with it.

Things aren't completely lost for the 'Briefcase Mong', despite the work-experience mix-up. Because as well as work-experience week it's also Valentine's Day and Charlotte 'Big Jugs' Hinchcliffe looks like she might be giving Will a second chance after their terrible sexual encounter. After receiving a bouquet of flowers from Will (smooth), 'Big Jugs' Hinchcliffe asks the younger Inbetweener to come along to an under-18s disco, where she's working behind the bar. This is perfect for his mate too, as Simon gets a Valentine's card off a girl in the year below who is also at the disco, so it looks like the pair of them could be in for a good night. So with a slight air of optimism, Will heads off to the garage, hoping things will all be sorted the following day and that he'll have his suit on in no time.

Things don't start well for the ex-public-school kid. After telling his colleague at the garage, 'No offence but I'm never going to work in a place like this... It's not that I'm better than this, it's just that I'm much cleverer than you need to be to work here,' the mechanics decide to get their own back by sending him on errands for supplies of tartan paint, spirit-level bubbles and a reach-around before throwing him into a lake. We love Will but reckon that, on this occasion, he deserved everything he got. Not so clever now, eh!

After running to his mum to sort his placement out, and still being told by Gilbert there's nothing that can be done, Will is forced to grit his teeth and troop on with the placement at the garage. Things start to go a little smoother for him and, on his last day, in an attempt to get one up on his fellow mechanics, he tells them about his 'romance' with Charlotte, adding much more than a pinch of salt to his story: 'She's fit, she's older than me and she goes like a porn star.' The only problem is that, instead of impressing them, 17-year-old garage-worker Wolfie (who looks about 30) tells Will he's going to come along to the junior disco to check Charlotte out himself!

This wasn't the smartest move Will had ever made and, when the night comes around, Charlotte finds out what he's been saying about her and pours a drink over him. Another chance squandered for Will, and Simon doesn't fare too much better either… mid-wank on the dance floor with the girl from the year below, a kid runs over and 'kicks him in the cock' to get him back for a previous altercation at school. So the lads finish the night hiding in the toilets while waiting for their parents to pick them up. Epic failure!

In the third episode of the series it looks like it's another outing for the gang, this time to sixth-former Louise Graham's 'Sexy Soirée'. And there's one extra to the 'awesome foursome' too: French exchange student Patrice, who's staying with Simon and his family for the week. Much cooler than the other lads, chain-smoking, leather-jacket-wearing Patrice doesn't seem to speak much English, apart from to tell Will, 'I've just had a really nice tug thinking about your mother. I think some went on the floor, sorry.'

Obviously, the lads haven't been invited to this party – after all, their recent antics haven't stood them in good stead for making any sort of good impression on the girls of Rudge Park Comp. Instead, Inbetweener Jay steals the invite from another girl's bag in school. But Will scuppers the plans, telling the others that his birthday is coming up and that he'd like to skip the soirée and host a dinner party at his!? The lads are less than impressed (not surprising really for a bunch of teenagers) but each is told they can bring a date, so they reluctantly go along with the plan for his sake.

The problem is that the night doesn't quite turn out as Will planned. With no girls, plenty of jokes about Will's 'Coq Au Vin', and revelations by Jay and Neil that they've ordered a stripper without any means to pay, the lads make a quick dart for Louise Graham's party, failing to ditch Patrice on the way.

However, when they arrive, it's only Patrice who is actually allowed into the party, with the others turned away because it's 'too busy'. Undeterred, they manage to scale a fence and, despite Will ending up in just a vest because his blazer has been covered in dog shit when crawling under the fence, they manage to finally get in.

The night ends in another fail for the lads though, topping off a terrible 17th birthday for Will, as he stumbles across long-term crush Charlotte Hinchcliffe in bed with Patrice. Not really the civilised birthday evening he'd hoped for!

The lads take their next big outing of the series in the fourth episode, 'A Night Out in London', when Will decides they need to ditch their current image and 'Carpe Diem'. The four agree that a trip to the capital's clubs is just what they need and, when love-of-Simon's-life Carli tells the gang that she and a mate are also going, the excitement builds up.

As per usual, things don't go the way the lads envisaged. The bad times start when Simon gets a throttling off a couple of fellas reacting to Jay shouting 'bus-wankers' at them as they drive past a bus stop. This is closely followed by Neil cutting the tip of his penis when trying to take a leak in a beer can, and then Simon having to swap his brand-new trainers with a tramp because the club has a 'shoes only' door policy. The failure of a night ends with none of the lads getting lucky: Neil is thrown out of the club, Simon's new trainers are filled with piss and the car is clamped. Standard stuff.

The final trip for the lads this series looks a little less exciting than previous adventures, as they head off to an old-people's home as part of the Duke of Edinburgh scheme. It's no surprise that the main motivation for the choice is a girl. This time Will finds out an old babysitter, Daisy, works at the home and, when the now-uni student takes a bit of a shine to him at a family party, he goes all out to make sure he gets his chance with her.

It looks like his plan is actually working when Daisy needs someone to cover one of her shifts. Will kindly offers the services of the gang, on the condition that she lets him take her for dinner. Unbelievably, she agrees!

Back at school, and with his hot date coming up, Will ends up falling asleep after all the hard work at the home. Neil and Jay take this golden opportunity to play a prank on Will, squirting a tube of hair-removal cream down his pants. After waking up and finding himself lacking the usual bodily hair, and in a fluster about his date, Will takes Simon's terrible advice of stuffing a wig down his pants and heads off to meet Daisy.

Unfortunately this time for Will, the date actually goes well and the pair end up back at Daisy's, where she eventually discovers the wig. Rethinking the idea that spending a night with Will is the right thing to do – and with the moment most definitely gone – poor Will's attempt to get a girl fails again.

The second series ends with one of our favourite episodes

ever, back in the confines of Rudge Park Comp, as the lads prepare – or don't prepare, as the case is for some – for the end of year AS-Level exams. Studious Will seems to be right on top of things from the off. He has a study timetable all mapped out, while Jay and Simon are more preoccupied with girls, as ever.

Jay has met and has started dating Chloe from another nearby school and Simon is keen to impress Carli (again), so has ditched his own revision to concentrate on tutoring her. Finally, there's Neil, with neither girls nor revision on his plate. Instead, he's been practising on Pro Evo in preparation for his PE exam!

Jay ends up scaring his new girlfriend away, Simon ends up planning resits and things come to a close for the series when Will, in his last exam, has a rather bad reaction to the excessive amount of energy drinks he's been consuming to help with the revision. And by bad reaction, we mean that the Inbetweener shits himself right in the middle of the exam hall. A great end to another failed term by the lads.

SERIES 3 – GIRLS, GIRLS, GIRLS AND TENTS

The third and final series starts with the boys returning to Rudge Park after the summer break and, as normal, a big part of their agenda is girls. Jay starts the new school year with one of his ears pierced, revealing that it's a ploy to get involved in the up-and-coming school fashion show. He explains his motives to the others by saying, 'When I'm up there modelling, I'll have the pick of the snatch.' Of course you will, Jay.

The piercing doesn't help his plan, however, and it's only Simon who is asked to model by organiser Carli, much to Jay's annoyance. Neil is less bothered though, as he's managed to secure a slot helping the models change during the show, so he can see 'some close-up flange for charity' – he thinks he's helping out in the girls' dressing room, but everyone else knows it's the boys' one.

It doesn't end well for any of the lads anyway, as Jay has an ear infection, Will is in Gilbert's bad books and Simon manages to walk down the stage for the grand finale with his bollock hanging out of his black Speedos. Nice!

Things do, however, start to look up for Simon in the second episode, 'Gig and the Girlfriend', when he convinces Tara (a girl in the year below) that he's a casual drug-taking, music-loving gig goer, despite a few initial hiccups…

'Cool, I love gigs,' says the girl. 'I went to a big gig last year; my mum took us to see Take That at Wembley Arena.'

When the night of the gig comes and the lads even eventually manage to get their hands on some weed after Jay's 'usual supplier' fails to materialise, chaos ensues: Simon manages to kiss Tara, despite her throwing up; Jay starts acting like a habitual drug user, even adding a Jamaican twang to his Essex accent; and Neil decides not to take the weed, instead opting for a cocktail of medicine and juice: 'Apparently if you mix them with Ribena, red wine and cough mixture, it gives you a well-good buzz.'

But worst off is definitely Will. After becoming annoyed with Jay, who's acting as if he's been taking drugs all of his life, Will takes nearly all the weed the gang purchased and eats it. This doesn't go down too well with the public-schoolboy and he soon needs help: 'You need to call an ambulance right now because I can't use the phone, my arms don't work and my hands are sausages… Listen, Simon, this is very important information: call an ambulance and tell them I'm in a bubble and everything is very flat. Look how random my arms are, help me… I need you to call me an ambulance or, failing that, my mummy, as I think I might be dead.'

When Will is finally carted off in an ambulance, the lads' first experience of a gig and drugs is done!

When he's over the drug-induced behaviour in the next episode of the series, Will receives another piece of bad news. Things have been going well for Simon and Tara and they've set Will up on a double-date with Tara's friend Kerry. Not at all keen on the idea at first, Will's mind is changed when he finds out that Kerry is partial to giving her boyfriends blow-jobs.

The thing Simon fails to point out, however, is that Kerry is a bit on the tall side and, when Will turns up for the date, she towers over him! Still, he sticks at it, keeping his mind focused on the potential 'blowy', and sees the date out until the end, even giving (or rather getting) a kiss at the end of the night.

So, after more deliberation, Will decides to invite the lofty Kerry to Inbetweener Neil's birthday party, even though he finds out she's changed her relationship status on Facebook to 'in a relationship'. But after some overly clingy behaviour on her part at the party, he eventually loses his rag, deciding that even he isn't desperate enough to put up with her and telling her he doesn't want to be her boyfriend, leaving Kerry in floods of tears before she heads off to give birthday-boy Neil a few blowjobs!

Will's insensitive treatment of 'Big Kerry' doesn't hamper Simon's chances with Tara though and, in fact, for once, things are looking good on the love front for one of the guys. So good, in fact, that it's looking like sex is on the cards for Si. Tara arranges for the pair to visit her sister, who's at university in Warwick, so they can have a bit of space away from parents and annoying kid brothers.

The other lads convince Simon that he needs to have a plan in place for the big night, including, 'For fuck's sake, don't wear a Johnny – it's a guaranteed hard-on killer – that's why they call it safe sex, 'cause you can't get it up.'

But rather than helping the nervous Simon, the terrible advice only makes him more apprehensive about the weekend, so much so that he invites Jay and Neil along on the trip to help get him through the 'event', with Will tagging along to check out Warwick's uni prospects (yawn).

When the group arrive, after a cramped journey made worse by Neil's 'Egg McMuffin' farts, the lads are pleased to find out that one of Tara's sister's flatmates is a Dutch girl and ideas start creeping into their minds that they may get a bit of action this weekend too.

Simon and Tara don't waste much time in getting down to business and, after some heavy petting and dry humping in the kitchen, they head upstairs. Simon decides that this is the perfect time to get some advice off the lads, as he's worried about controlling his 'excitement', so Jay tells him that the best thing to do is to quickly 'knock one out' in the bathroom before getting down to anything with Tara.

Why he's listening to 'bullshitter Jay' is anyone's guess but Simon follows the terrible advice and it works too well because, when he's back in the bedroom with Tara, his excitement is more than under control; he can't get it up at all! Simon ends up frantically punching his penis in a desperate attempt to stimulate any sort of response: 'Why won't you get big? Oh, please just work, you ugly cunt!' But the less-than-impressed Tara runs out of the room and the gang are kicked out of the house, forced to sleep in their little yellow car, before Tara texts Si to end their short-lived relationship.

THE LEGACY

After a number of failed trips away, home seems like a pretty safe place for the lads in the fifth episode of the third series and, when Will's mum tells the lads she's off for a weekend away with 'an old friend' she's caught up with on Facebook, a free house sounds perfect to the gang (besides Will, who is unimpressed to say the least about the thought of his mum and a stranger having a dirty trip away).

Still, the weekend starts off like clockwork for the foursome. Neil tells the boys he's going to 'have a wank' over Will's mum that night and Jay decides to vandalise a few flower beds. Next on the agenda is a 'pussy patrol' (an unlicensed and uninsured drive around the block in Jay's mum's car in which they run over a squirrel), blocking the toilet, a few beers and some more garden vandalism, this time involving Simon's golf clubs.

After this particularly heavy night – not what Will had planned at all – the lads wake up to a furious man banging on the front door of the house – it turns out that it was the neighbour's flower beds they were wrecking. After plenty of hiding and some arguing, it takes the return of Will's mum to calm down the situation and the lads, again, end up in plenty of trouble after plans that got a bit out of hand!

The final series ends with big news for a couple of the gang. Simon is called to a family meeting, where his folks explain that they all need to move to Swansea for his dad's work, and Neil receives a text from 'saucy ASDA Karen' telling him she 'Did the test. It's positive. Thought you should know :/'.

Will decides a camping trip is just what the lads need to cheer them up and, although Jay has his reservations about the countryside on account of the cows 'spraying milk from their tits', and Simon wants to spend his last few weeks with Carli,

THE INBETWEENERS

Will gets his own way and the gang head off to camp at a lake in the forest, Monopoly in tow.

After an emotional poo, petrol-doused fire, some texting campfire games and Simon's car rolling into the lake, the trip comes to an end and the four are left walking home.

CHAPTER TWO

THE REAL INBETWEENERS

Since landing back in the UK after the filming of one of the best-received British comedy films ever (*The Inbetweeners Movie*, if that wasn't obvious), the cast have been busy on loads of exciting projects. In fact, it's been difficult turning on the TV or radio, opening a paper or having a mooch on Twitter without Joe Thomas (Simon Cooper), Simon Bird (Will McKenzie), Blake Harrison (Neil Sutherland) or James Buckley (Jay Cartwright) popping up!

And it's not only the awesome foursome whose profiles have been boosted by the movie's massive success.

The show and the film have put others into the limelight too, including Emily Head (Carli D'Amato), Emily Atack (Charlotte Hinchcliffe), Belinda Stewart-Wilson (Will's mum) and everyone's favourite Head of Sixth Form, Greg Davies (Mr Gilbert), as well as newbies who come into the boys' adventures in the first film: Laura Haddock (Alison), Tamla Kari (Lucy), Jessica Knappett (Lisa) and Lydia Rose Bewley (Jane).

In this section we'll delve into the lives of the actors behind your favourite characters, finding out where it all started for them, what they've been up to and more. Enjoy!

THE AWESOME FOURSOME

James Buckley

Before *The Inbetweeners*
Born and raised in London, James Buckley quickly got the acting bug. He was only seven when he started attending a stage school at weekends and by the age of eleven he got his first professional gig in West End shows *Whistle Down the Wind* and *Les Misérables* – a far cry from the filthy character he was to play a few years later!

Career
As well as his early acting credits on the stage, before his breakthrough role as Inbetweener Jay Cartwright, Buckley appeared in several well-known TV shows, including *Teachers* (2004), *Holby City* (2006), *Skins* (2007) and *The Bill* (2005, 2006, 2008).

It wasn't until *The Inbetweeners* though that Buckley got his big break as he launched onto our screens as foul-mouthed bullshitting Jay Cartwright, and his acting in this role was recognised at the highest level when he was nominated for British Comedy Award for Best Comedy Actor (2010), the BAFTA for Best Male Performance in a Comedy Role (2011) and the Royal Television Society Award for Best Comedy Performance (2011). Unfortunately, Buckley didn't win.

Other TV Work

Since *The Inbetweeners* hit our screens, Buckley's acting credits have continued to grow. He's had main roles in the BBC3 show *Off the Hook*, which follows a group of freshers as they embark on student life in their first year at Bankside University, and the BBC1 prequel to the British comedy institution *Only Fools and Horses*: *Rock & Chips*.

You will have also heard Buckley's voice pop up on several commercials and he's even provided backing vocals and guitar on ex-Ocean Colour Scene guitarist Steve Cradock's album *Peace City West*, showing he's certainly more than a one-trick pony!

Other Film Work

It's not just as Jay Cartwright that Buckley has managed to get onto the big screen. In 2011 Buckley had a small role in British coming-of-age drama *Everywhere and Nowhere*, acting alongside up-and-coming actor James Floyd, and Simon Webbe of Blue.

Next for Buckley was the 2013 film *Charlie Countrymen*, starring young Hollywood heavyweight Shia LaBeouf alongside Harry Potter's Rupert Grint. The film wasn't a hit with critics but it can definitely be seen as a positive for the *Inbetweeners* star, who's quickly gaining big-screen experience alongside some massive names in the industry. A source told the *Sun* newspaper how the star had hoped his experience would start landing him more juicy roles:

'James hoped *The Inbetweeners Movie* would lead to bigger things – but this is pretty impressive.

'He fitted the mould of the character perfectly and was the outstanding choice. It's a big chance to establish himself in Hollywood.'

It didn't stop there for the young star either. Buckley also revealed on Twitter (@James_Buckley) that he'd tried to bag himself a part in the Steve Coogan hit *Alpha Papa*.

'I read for a part in *Alpha Papa*. Embarrassingly, I'm such a Coogan geek I was literally star struck (sic) of the script. Was V nervous, I wasn't cast.'

This didn't put him off the film, however, with Buckley tweeting after the movie's release: 'Who has seen *Alpha Papa*! God, I want to see it so bad,' soon followed by: 'Off to see alpha papa this afternoon with my wife for my birthday!'

We reckon Buckley would have been brilliant in this film but are glad he took this one on the chin and still got out to see the Coogan classic!

Did You Know?

Ocean Colour Scene guitarist Steve Cradock is close friends with James and his wife Clair, and godfather to the couple's first baby, Harrison Buckley.

It was rumoured that the arrival was named after *Inbetweeners* co-star Blake Harrison (Neil) but, reading into Clair Buckley's tweets, we reckon it's probably more likely to be someone else, with her tweeting a picture of Beatle George Harrison along with the message, 'Happy Birthday to my firstborn's name sake. My favourite'

Simon Bird

Simon Bird was born in Surrey on 19 August 1984 with what

can be best described as a middle-class upbringing and you would imagine not too far from that of his alter-ego Will McKenzie! Simon has two brothers and a sister and they were brought up by their parents, Heather and Graham Bird, in Guildford in Surrey, a town around 25 miles from London.

Before *The Inbetweeners*

During his youth, Simon attended the Royal Grammar School in Guildford, a school that requires an annual fee and one for which the students need to pass an entrance exam to gain entry; however, there are scholarships available for music, arts and academic achievement. Without a scholarship, fees for the school are around £13,000 per year. Former pupils of the Royal Grammar School include sports commentator Martin Tyler, Monty Python's Terry Jones and England cricketing legend Bob Willis! After making his way through school, Simon then found himself at the prestigious Queens College at Cambridge University, where he would read English. The Queens College at Cambridge has many famous former students, most notably English actor and comedian Stephen Fry (it seems that a dry wit is a must-have at Queens College!). Other former students of Queens College include Oscar-nominated film director Paul Greengrass and a host of politicians, writers and royal dignitaries from around the world.

After completing his degree Bird studied for an MA at Birkbeck, University of London, which is located in Bloomsbury and has been the educational institution for many economists, writers and politicians.

Career

Cambridge is where Simon Bird's comedy career started to form when he joined the famous Footlights, a theatrical club run by the students. Footlights was formed in 1883 and since that date the club has been performing regular sketch shows and stand-up comedy events. The Footlights society has a rich history and throughout the years it has been the breeding ground for many young, up-and-coming British comedians. Famous Footlights alumni include David Baddiel, John Cleese, Hugh Dennis, Stephen Fry and Eric Idle, to name a few.

While at Birkbeck, Bird set up the sketch-comedy outfit 'The House of Windsor' with Joe Thomas and Jonny Sweet, and in 2007 and 2008 they played at the Edinburgh Fringe Festival. Steve Bennett of *Chortle* reviewed the act back in 2007: 'Simon Bird, Jonny Sweet and Joe Thomas are certainly a stylish act, and will probably appeal to the sensibilities of a Radio 4 listener who demands their comedy with class. This may be the first time we've heard of them as a trio, but it surely won't be the last.' Steve, how right you were! In 2006 and 2007 Simon Bird and Joe Thomas were also regulars on *The Weekly Show*, a Channel 4 Radio podcast. However, Channel 4 Radio was only in commission from January 2007–October 2008.

Along with sketch shows, Simon has also tried his hand at stand-up comedy and took part in *Chortle*'s student comedy awards in 2005, 2006, 2007 and 2008. In 2007 Bird was controversially disqualified from the competition in dubious circumstances after he was asked by the sponsors of the competition, 'Revels', not to mention any other confectionery snack. Not being one to play by the rules, Simon went on to mention a raft of chocolate bars throughout his act! When returning in 2008 Simon made light of the disqualification, stating, 'No one, but no one tells the Bird man he can't talk about confectionery!'

In 2008, the big break came for Bird when Damon Beesley and Iain Morris watched one of the sketch shows in Edinburgh and asked both him and Joe Thomas to audition for a new comedy they were writing called *The Inbetweeners*. After that, the rest is history! Simon would go on to win Best Male Newcomer at the 2008 British Comedy Awards and Best Actor at the 2009 British Comedy Awards. Not bad for a posh boy from Surrey, we think! There's certainly more to come from Simon in acting and writing. Find out what's ahead in the section entitled 'The Future'.

Blake Harrison

Blake Harrison is best known for playing our beloved and dim-witted Neil Sutherland in *The Inbetweeners*. He was born on 23 June 1985 in Greenwich, London.

Before *The Inbetweeners*

Blake attended the famous Brit School in 2003, a school in Croydon, England, which has been the breeding ground for many aspiring actors and performers over the years. The school is free to attend for all of those invited and accepted after an interview or audition. It is funded by the British Government and has support from the British Record Industry Trust. Many famous alumni have trodden the boards at The Brit School, including singers Adele, Leona Lewis, Amy Winehouse, Jessie J and a host of other stars of the stage and screen.

After The Brit School, Blake attended East 15 Acting School

based in Loughton, Essex, where he would graduate and further his career in acting. East 15 offers degrees and master's degrees in many subjects, including BA Acting on its own, BA Acting and Contemporary Theatre and MA/MFA Filmmaking. Notable alumni of the East 15 School include Marcus Bentley (the famous voice of reality-TV show *Big Brother!*). Blake, you're in great company!

Career

After finishing his education, Blake found his first acting role, like many young actors, in the ITV police drama *The Bill*. Not something to be scoffed at, the series ran from 1984–2010 and has spring-boarded the careers of many famous actors and actresses, including Robert Carlyle, David Tenant, Russell Brand and Keira Knightley. Blake made two appearances as the character of Pete Monks in 2008.

It was in 2007 when Blake would get his first big break and claim the character we know and love today, Neil Sutherland. Blake attended an open audition for the part, an experience he is quoted as describing as a 'cattle market' when trying to get seen with all the out-of-work actors that had turned up. Fortunately, writers Damon Beesley and Iain Morris picked him out of the crowd, invited him back for a second audition and offered him the part.

While filming *The Inbetweeners* between the years of 2008–10, Blake also took part in other projects, most notably a viral video that appeared on the Facebook page of the deodorant brand Lynx, which was called *Keeping Keeley*: an interactive film where the user gets to choose the next scene. Blake played the part of Jack, who attempts to win over actress and glamour model Keeley Hazell, who takes him into some strange and provocative places. Lads, this is well worth a watch on YouTube and Blake, you're one lucky guy! In between filming for *The Inbetweeners Movie* Blake also appeared in the BBC3 sitcom *Him & Her* as the character of Barney for two episodes, namely 'The Rollover' (the episode where the main couple, Steve and Becky, invite a host of people around to the flat for the rollover lottery draw) and 'The Football' (Steve invites his friends around to watch the big game, only to be constantly interrupted by Becky's sister Laura).

Since the first *Inbetweeners* film, Blake has gone on to portray a range of characters and has even tried his hand at theatre acting. You can find out more about his various work in the section 'Life After The Inbetweeners.'

Twitter

Outside of his acting, Blake is an avid Twitter user and, to date, has over 103,000 followers and has tweeted over 3,000 times – pretty impressive! Among his most tweeted subjects are his beloved Millwall Football Club, upcoming projects and, of course, his long-term girlfriend Kerry-Ann Lynch. As one of the most active Twitter users in our *Inbetweeners* bunch, we thought we'd give you a taste of some @blakeharrison23's best tweets:

'Thanks Australia! We've had a great time filming here. Hopefully be back soon. P.s. can I take your weather with me?' After finishing shooting in Australia, Blake reflects on the time the lads had there.

'Really happy with Holloway. Gonna be a hard task but I think weve got a great manager!#millwall #veryfewofyouwill careaboutthistweet.' One of the many tweets about Millwall

FC! Blake looks forward to life with new manager Ian Holloway and recognises that not many of his followers will be that bothered!

'Things better about Oz: 1. The bananas here are massive! Properly massive! (This is not a euphemism) 2. Premiership games r always on!' While on location in Australia, the *Inbetweeners* star makes some observations!

'A few people saying my old episode of the bill is on. Got to wave a gun around & act like a gangsta! Not sure why that casting didn't stick?' Reflecting on old times, Blake recalls his first acting job on *The Bill*.

'Trying to annoy my gf by loudly singing Pure Morning in an exaggerated Placebo style. She hasn't reacted at all. It's really frustrating.' One of many tweets about his girlfriend Kerry-Ann.

'Quick! Make a cup of tea! Have a poo! Maybe get a cheeky wank in? But do it now coz #BigBadWorld starts in 10 mins On Comedy Central!' Some advice from Blake before settling down to watch *Big Bad World*.

'Thanks to my loyal followers who watched #bigbadworld! To u disloyal followers we WILL find you! We WILL make you sniff miley's foam finger!' Blake thanks his loyal followers after his latest project airs and dishes out a severe warning to those who didn't watch it!

Other TV Work

Blake has made several appearances on popular UK television shows, such as Channel 4's *Sunday Brunch*, a Sunday-morning TV show hosted by Tim Lovejoy and Simon Rimmer, where guests make casual banter with the hosts then make a delicious dish or two; *Alan Carr: Chatty Man*, where Blake appeared with other members of *The Inbetweeners* in 2010 and 2011 to chat about the series and enjoy a drink with the comedian; *BBC Breakfast*, where the guys met with Bill Turnbull and Louise Minchin for a chat about *The Inbetweeners Movie*; and several other TV movie-documentary 'countdown'-style programmes, with Blake talking about his love for his favourite shows – for example, *Family Guy: The Top 20 Characters*, a BBC3 show celebrating the stars of the risqué cartoon comedy.

Joe Thomas
Before *The Inbetweeners*
Born in Chelmsford, Essex on 28 October 1983, Thomas had a 'normal' life as a kid. A bit of a bright spark from the off, Joe attended the prestigious King Edward VI Grammar School during his teenage years.

Joe says that, while at KEGS, and unlike his *Inbetweeners* character Simon Cooper, he was not so hopeless with girls because he did not know many.

He told the *Essex Chronicle*:

What I most remember of KEGS was the debating club or what became the Fleur-de-lis comedy club. I don't know why it became as such but it became a comedy club by proxy. It was a club for making jokes. We referred to them as debates but we used it to show off jokes.

At school girls were just not my life. I made a point of falling in love with every girl I met because I probably knew about five. I worked pretty hard at school and looked young so couldn't get served [in pubs]. Simon was a failure with girls but I would have loved to have failed but I wasn't even in the game. Simon's sulkiness I had though and his tendency to over-dramatise everything.

Like on-screen character Simon Cooper, Joe wasn't the coolest kid at school and was certainly no rebel, admitting to being even less adventurous than the Inbetweener:

The one time I got served underage I went back to the same man and didn't get served. Like the show, we did always get Stella. We thought, if we asked for a Stella, they would think we were worldlier but I spent more time playing football manager.

So Simon is worldlier than I was, which is humiliating. I wasn't out and about very much. I did have friends but I didn't just 'hang out'. I didn't go out aimlessly waiting for something to happen because I knew that nothing was going to happen.

And probably to the relief of Joe's parents, he managed to avoid the Joey Essex/Mario Falcone/James Argent TOWIE permi-tan and bleached teeth, instead opting to pack his bags for the University of Cambridge to read History at Pembroke College. This is where the story of Joe's career starts.

He did well academically, achieving a 2:1 degree in History in 2006 but we're not too sure how good Joe would have been as a historian and it doesn't look like he was too keen on the studying side of uni either: 'I never really recovered from the fact that the lecturers weren't paid to be nice to me. Or that the carrot-and-stick thing that happened at school no longer occurred. If you do quite well, nobody's that bothered; and if you really fuck up, nobody's that bothered. It has to be from you and I was easily distracted.'

All was not lost though, as it was at Cambridge where Joe's comedy pedigree first shone through, serving as the president and secretary of Footlights, the famous Cambridge Universtiry Footlights Dramatic Club, that's helped nurture the comedy genius of greats such as Clive Anderson, David Baddiel, John Cleese, Stephen Fry and Eric Idle, and was the starting block for loads of great comedy partnerships, including Mitchell and Webb, Armstrong and Miller, The Goodies and the team who made Monty Python!

Cambridge University Footlights Dramatic Club gave Thomas a real taste for performance and he acted alongside other University of Cambridge students at the Edinburgh Festival Fringe in a production of William Shakespeare's classic comedy play, *All's Well That Ends Well*.

Not only did he get a real taste for the stage at Footlights, Thomas also met a couple of fellow students who would be key to his career: Jonny Sweet & Simon Bird (aka Will of *The Inbetweeners* fame).

Maybe not a name you're familiar with (yet), Jonny Sweet also studied at Pembroke College, Cambridge, where he, too, became a member of Footlights. He served under Simon Bird as Vice President when Thomas was secretary and the three quick-witted students quickly became friends.

They ended up sharing a flat together and, as comedy ideas began bouncing around between the three, it only made sense that they should start putting pen to paper, so they became writing partners.

Career

Joe's big break was the first series of *The Inbetweeners*. As Simon Cooper, over the next three series Joe got into some outrageously funny situations, including a road trip to Thorpe Park, where he managed to wreck his brand-new (old) Fiat Cinquecento 'Hawaii Edition', and a fashion show at school, where he managed to show the entire sixth form his bollock! And since becoming involved in the hit show, his career has skyrocketed.

Other TV Work

After filming finished on *The Inbetweeners*, Joe didn't get much of a break work-wise. The young actor's next big role was as one of the stars of the Channel 4 hit show *Fresh Meat*, where Joe plays student Kingsley. And Joe has admitted that his next role reflected his student life much more than *The Inbetweeners* did, telling the *Radio Times*: 'I was quite similar to Kingsley. I thought it was a cool thing to be good at your work and I really wanted to succeed.'

As well as this main role in *Fresh Meat*, Joe somehow found time to co-write a new sitcom *Chickens* with fellow Inbetweener Simon Bird (Will) and writing partner Jonny Sweet. Just like he'd done with his previous roles, the talented comedy actor gives a brilliant and witty performance in his TV writing debut.

Other Film Work

It's not just the *Inbetweeners* movies that Joe's been involved with either. He already has two more short films under his belt: *A Trick of the Light* and *Straw Donkey*. With some class roles already to his name, we can't wait to see what Joe is involved in next: whether it's TV, film or writing, it's bound to be top notch!

Personal Life

Thomas does well at keeping his head out of the press, other than for the usual promo stuff for upcoming projects. He did have a dabble with Twitter in 2012 but has since closed his account, opting for a quiet life out of the limelight. It's probably for the best, Joe, as we all want to see some more of your work!

He has found love though and it was actually on the set of the third series of *The Inbetweeners*. In the second episode of the series, 'The Gig and The Girlfriend', Joe's onscreen character Simon gets talking to Tara, a girl in the year below him, played by Hannah Tointon. In the show, Simon ends up dragging the lads along to a gig to impress the girl and it works for a short time. You can find out more about Hannah in the section 'The Inbetweeners' Other Halves'.

Did You Know?

Joe Thomas isn't the Inbetweener in his family. In fact, he's the oldest, with three younger brothers underneath him. We reckon Joe would make a great big brother although, after seeing his character Simon's onscreen romantic mishaps, maybe not!

When Simon Cooper tried to impress love of his life Carli D'Amato by spray-painting a mural on her front drive, maybe he would have been better off using some of real-life Joe Thomas's romancing skills. Actor Thomas is great on the guitar and violin, and maybe a soothing love song might have given his onscreen character a better chance!

A bright spark from an early age, Thomas was a member of the Chelmsford school team that built T.R.A.C.I.E., a grand-finalist robot in the first series of *Robot Wars*.

THE INBETWEENERS' OTHER HALVES

Lisa Owens – Mrs Simon Bird

Simon Bird married his long-time uni girlfriend Lisa Owens, whom he met at university, in the summer of 2012. He popped the question while in Paris and a year later they were hitched.

On his stag party in Cambridge, Bird tells the *Mirror* about the moment his co-star in *The Inbetweeners*, Joe Thomas, ended up in the river:

> There were 14 of us and, this is going to make us sound really posh, but we were punting and somebody recognised Joe. They leapt on to his punt from the bank and wrestled the punt stick out of his hands. They hugged him and said, 'I think it is time for us to go in the river.' Joe said, 'Is it?' and in they went.

Even though Simon is a happily married man, he says that it still doesn't stop the female admirers:

> When it comes to female-fan attention, I'm married, so obviously I avoid the places where you might get unwanted female attention – clubs and social environments, bars and public spaces. I don't go out on the pull but sometimes girls will approach me in the street and say they like my work and would I like to go for a drink and I'll say thank you very much, but no.

Clair Meek – Mrs James Buckley

Off-screen, Buckley seems to be a lot more mature than

Inbetweener Jay. Rather than spending his time coming up with tales about orgies and the like, he's much more grown up.

In fact, the young star is married! This comes as a surprise to many who think of Buckley as the immature Jay he plays onscreen but his wife Clair Meek, former *FHM* High Street Honey and glamour model, told the *Daily Mail* how different he is to his most popular character: 'He's very respectful. He didn't come out with any outrageous chat-up lines. James doesn't need to stretch the truth as he's doing so well anyway.'

James Buckley married Scottish lass Clair Meek in November 2012 in a castle outside Edinburgh. They currently have two sons together, Harrison and Jude. James's co-stars from *The Inbetweeners*, Simon Bird, Joe Thomas and Blake Harrison, were all invited to the ceremony.

This certainly doesn't sound like Buckley's immature on-screen counterpart and in October 2011 the pair took the biggest step with the birth of their first baby, Harrison.

They couldn't contain their excitement, with the *Inbetweeners* star telling the *Sun*, 'Clair and I wanted to let everyone know we are having a baby. Chuffed to say it's going brilliantly. All very exciting with the film out in August and baby out soon after that. Can't quite believe my luck. Didn't think I had it in me.'

Buckley told *Whatsontv.co.uk* how the news was a shock to some fans:

I can't wait; it's going to be really cool. It's like the longest Christmas Eve ever. I'm going to be hands on and stuff.'

I think people were really confused when news got out that I was having a baby. What – Jay from *The Inbetweeners*, a 17-year-old foul-mouthed boy?

Obviously I'm a man in my mid-twenties and have an apartment and a girlfriend and live a very normal life.

But on the arrival of their bundle of joy, a friend of the couple told the *Sun* newspaper, 'They are the happiest people in the world. They are so thrilled and proud. The two of them are so in love and now they have a beautiful baby son.'

The baby was a hit with the other *Inbetweeners* guys too, with Simon Bird who plays Will McKenzie telling the *Sun*, 'We met the little bastard the other day and he is a little bastard, technically. But I can honestly say he's the cutest thing I've ever seen in my life – he's really sweet.'

And in 2012 Buckley revealed more exciting news for the couple, tweeting, 'Baby scan today. I feel like I should make an effort & dress nice to promote a "good dad" vibe. Any other expectant dads get this paranoid?' followed soon by, 'It's another boy that will be joining the family! i am very pleased to share my exciting news with you all :) J x RT.'

The couple's second child, another boy, Jude, was born in August 2013. There's no word yet from the pair as to whether or not they're planning a third but, with James admitting once to the *Sun* that he does want a girl, we reckon it might be on the cards for the young couple!

Did You Know?
James wore a kilt to honour his new bride's Scottish roots. What would Jay think about a man wearing a skirt, I wonder?!

Hannah Tointon – Miss Joe Thomas
Joe has been dating Hannah Tointon since they met on the set

of *The Inbetweeners* in 2010. Hannah played the character of Tara, Simon's love interest in the series, and the pair had to share a number of embarrassing scenes together, so it's fair to say they got to know each other well before they starting dating for real!

It has been widely reported in the press that Joe and Hannah share a flat in central London. However, there are no rumours of wedding bells just yet. In fact, Hannah has been reported to have said that she won't get married until big sister Kara (also an actress) ties the knot with her *Strictly Come Dancing* boyfriend Artem Chigvinstev.

Hannah is most famous for playing the character of Katy Fox in the Channel 4 soap opera *Hollyoaks*. However, along with starring in *The Inbetweeners*, Hannah's other acting credits include supernatural comedy drama *Switch*, BBC drama series *The Hour* and TV series *Midsomer Murders, Death in Paradise* and *Call the Midwife*.

Kerry-Ann Lynch – Miss Blake Harrison

Blake has been dating Kerry-Ann Lynch for a number of years. Kerry works in PR and is regularly seen on Blake Harrison's twitter feed as he regularly refers to her as 'the ginger', due to her having red hair, obviously! Kerry, who is also an avid Twitter user, has a couple of hundred followers and often promotes Blake's upcoming shows and tweets James Buckley's wife Clair on occasion.

In an interview with *Metro* in 2010, Blake gave some advice to the readers about how to woo the ladies: 'Listening to them's always good, they'll ask you about things later. It's like an exam, they don't like it if you forget things. I'm not bad on first dates, it's keeping them interested longer than a week that's my problem.' Blake also went on to describe what he was like in school and if he was ever lucky in love in his youth: 'I was very much an Inbetweener type. I spent most of my time playing computer games. I was a hopeless romantic and I'm still like that now – I'd instantly fall in love with any girl who'd pay me any attention. I was constantly moping around after girls.'

Well, Blake, luckily by the sound of things, you're not as dim-witted as your character Neil in *The Inbetweeners*, who mistakenly thought he had 'knocked up' 'Saucy ASDA Karen' in the final ever episode – well… at least, we hope you're not as dim-witted as him!

CHAPTER THREE

OTHER CAST & CREW MEMBERS

Greg Davies

A little bit longer in the tooth than the other cast members of *The Inbetweeners*, you'd expect Greg to have a lot more experience than his co-stars.

In fact, it wasn't until Greg was in his thirties that he got into comedy because the *Inbetweeners*' Head of Sixth was actually a real-life teacher! And thankfully, it sounds like he wasn't as scary as Mr Gilbert. Here's Greg telling the *Radio Times* how he was quite popular with the pupils:

I had one buttock-clenchingly embarrassing moment when the head called me in to tell me one of my pupils had nominated me for the prestigious Teacher of the Year award. The pupil had to fill in four pages of documentation but on the form she had simply written one thing. It said, 'Mr Davies is a well good laugh and he don't make us do no work.' The head wiped away tears of laughter before throwing the form in the bin.

Career

After deciding to follow his dream of comedy, thanks to some pushing from his girlfriend, Greg started working the comedy circuit and was soon being recognised for his talent by his peers. He was nominated for three *Chortle* Awards for his part in the three-piece comedy show We Are Klang including Breakthrough Actor, Best Sketch, Variety or Character Act and Best Full-Length Show.

With his career on the up, *The Inbetweeners* came at the perfect time for Greg and the three series and first film shot the comedian to stardom, helping him get regular spots on panel shows and comedy programmes.

Other TV Work

Things didn't stop there for the talented comedian and actor. After his appearance in *The Inbetweeners Movie*, Greg moved on to star in *Cuckoo* alongside fellow *Inbetweeners* star Tamla Kari, as her onscreen dad in the BBC Three hit.

Next on the agenda for Greg was co-writing and starring in sitcom *Man Down*. And it seems he keeps going back to teaching in some form, as Greg explained to *The Guardian* how the hit show, which follows a teacher unhappy with his work life, is loosely based on his own time behind the desk at the front of a classroom:

My family and ex-colleagues in the teaching profession will be delighted when I put on the record that very few of the incidents that happen in *Man Down* actually happened in real life but there is a more general truth to it. I wrote about a time when I was totally lost at sea and I just took the humiliation of my character, Dan, to a more extreme place. My mum said, 'Anyone watching this will think you grew up in a mad house.' I did. We all did.

And as well as building his career on the small screen, the new star has also managed to keep his hand in stand-up, with his smash-hit tour The Back Of My Mum's Head Live. The hilarious show was very well received by critics, with *The Guardian* describing it as 'A joyous celebration of our shared idiocy and a snook cocked at self-importance'.

Things look to be going from strength to strength for the actor and comedian, who's showing the world that you never have to give up on your dream. Well done, Greg, we love you!!!

Did You Know?

There's a blog solely dedicated to the sex symbol that is Greg Davies. Greg Davies Sexual Frustration: *gdsexual frustration.tumblr.com* chronicles one fan's love for all things Greg as they describe their passion for the comedian: 'I'm entirely convinced that Greg Davies is the sexiest man alive. He's tall, he has a pretty face, he's hilarious and he comes with his own preexisting teacher kink. Stop, just come and confess.'

Yes, he's a dapper-looking gentleman but, come on, this is probably just a few steps too far. Isn't it?!

Emily Head

Background

Emily Head, aka Carli D'Amato in *The Inbetweeners*, was born in London on 15 December 1988. Her father is Anthony Head, who is probably most famous for being the Gold Blend man in the Nescafé adverts during the 1990s, and he played the part of Rupert Giles in the American TV series *Buffy the Vampire Slayer*. He also played the part of Will's father in *The Inbetweeners Movie*.

During her youth, Emily trained at the Dorothy Colebourne School of Dance, a school in Bath founded in 1920, and one which over the years has raised many thousands of pounds for local charities. She then went on to study theatre at the Brit School, the same school where fellow Inbetweener Blake Harrison would ply his trade.

Career

It was in 2005 that Emily would receive her first major acting credit in the Lynda La Plante police drama *Trial & Retribution*. Emily played the part of Natalie Franke in the episode 'The Lovers: Part 1'. In 2007 she then got a small role in the comedy drama series *Doc Martin* alongside Martin Clunes. The premise of the show followed Clunes as Dr Martin Ellingham trying to make his way as a GP in a small Cornish village. Emily played the part of Poppy in the episode 'Movement'.

In 2008 Emily starred alongside her father in the comedy drama series *The Invisibles*. The show revolved around two retired burglars who return to the UK from a life on the run in the Mediterranean only to succumb to a life of crime again. Emily plays Maurice's (played by Anthony Head) daughter Grace. The show only aired for one series of six episodes.

OTHER CAST & CREW MEMBERS

After getting the role of Carli in *The Inbetweeners*, from 2010 Emily found herself in the British BBC soap *Doctors*, the series following the lives of staff of a medical practice in a fictional town in the Midlands. Emily played the part of Liz Wates in the episode 'An Unexpected Arrival'.

The next project Emily undertook was in 2010 with *William & Catherine: A Royal Romance*, an American television movie depicting the relationship between Prince William and Kate Middleton during their days at St Andrews University, and subsequently William's army training and their Royal Wedding plans. Emily played the part of Cynthia in the movie, which was shot in Budapest.

Other TV Work

In 2012 Emily was to feature in the American TV series *Robot Chicken*, an animated series where she played a number of voices, including 'Bella Swan' and 'Mary Poppins'. The series is a Claymation comedy series created by Seth Green (of *Family Guy* fame) and Matthew Senreich (an American screenwriter, director and TV producer). Along with Emily Head, the show has seen many celebrity guest voices, including 50 Cent, Daniel Radcliffe, David Hasselhoff, Jean-Claude Van Damme and Whoopi Goldberg, to name a few.

Whatever happens to Emily, we'll always love her for playing Carli and it's fair to say that it's been her biggest role to date. However, she told the *Daily Mail* how much she still can't believe the success of the show:

If anyone had told us four years ago that we'd be doing a movie version of *The Inbetweeners*, we'd have laughed in their face. But I guess the show is so loved because it's true to life. In some ways, it's the anti-*Skins*; this is what the teenage experience is really like, in all its messy, fumbling, clueless chaos. But the biggest surprise is that parents enjoy it as much as their kids and they watch it together. I guess everyone remembers being at school and they can identify with one or another of the characters and their problems and longings and highs and lows. We've all been there. I think some people still are… That's a chilling thought!

Twitter

Although not an avid Twitter user, Emily has over 5,200 followers on the social-media network, where she mostly tweets her latest news or responds to her latest followers. Let's take a look at some of the Tweet highlights from @emily_head:

'Home Alone 2 on tv, chocolate snowmen in the local shop. It's September. It's not even winter yet. This is getting out of hand.' Emily looks forward to Christmas…in September!

'If you fancy a bit of theatre go to 9 steps (of 12) at Trafalgar Studios. Starring the very talented @blakeharrison23, he's brilliant.' A massive 'big-up' to *Inbetweeners* pal Blake Harrison.

'So I've failed miserably to keep my resolution. Already. Off on holiday now so hopefully there will be lots of interesting things to tweet!' Emily reflects on her New Year's resolution to start tweeting more, and failing!

'Just wanted to send a massive thank you for all the lovely messages from all the lovely people over the last couple of weeks. Thank you! Xxx' Thanking the fans after the release of *The Inbetweeners Movie*.

Henry Lloyd-Hughes

Henry Lloyd-Hughes is probably most famous for playing the high-school bully Mark Donovan in *The Inbetweeners*. However, he has also now turned his hand to writing and producing along with other high-profile acting credits. He's come a long way since coining the phrase 'Bender Squad!'

Background

Henry was born in August 1985 in London and comes from an acting family. His brother is Ben Lloyd-Hughes, an actor whose credits include *Skins*, *The Hour* and *Great Expectations*. His mother is Lucy Appleby and his grandfather is Basil Appleby. Lucy played many acting roles in the 1960s and 1970s and is best known for films *A Stitch in Time* (1963) and *Ballad in Blue* (1964). Basil Appleby was an actor, producer and production manager on a number of film and TV shows from the early 1940s to the mid-1990s. His production credits include *The Adventures of Black Beauty* and *Walt Disney's Wonderful World of Color*.

Henry was educated at St Paul's School in London, which is described as one of the leading educational establishments in the country and one which has the highest acceptance rate into Oxford or Cambridge Universities. However, it was to be a different route that Henry would choose – a career in acting. After finishing school he chose not to go to university. Instead, he signed with an agency with a view to auditioning for acting roles while working to pay the bills. Of course, it wasn't going to be easy finding acting work and Henry told *The Independent* in an interview in 2013 that the experience has shaped who he is today:

If you exist in a closed world, you can become incredibly blinkered. If you're blinkered, you've got nothing coming in. That was what I told myself at the time anyway. The number of different situations I've been in – working in a bar, clearing up people's sick at four in the morning when I hadn't slept and hadn't had a break. I don't want to make it sound as if I was down the mines because I wasn't but it was a reminder of real life.

Threatening to give it all in while working as a landscape gardener, Henry bought a ticket to Asia, presumably with a view to seeing more of the world, when his agent called with his first real break.

Career

Henry Lloyd-Hughes's first major acting role came in 2004, playing the part of 'Jenson Dawlish' in the TV series *Murphy's Law*, a drama series starring James Nesbitt as an undercover police officer. It was soon after *Murphy's Law* that Henry would find himself in front of the big screen and in 2005 he played the character of Roger Davies in the fourth Harry Potter film, *Harry Potter and the Goblet of Fire*. The acting roles were now coming in thick and fast and he would find himself in the CBBC show *M.I. High* and the TV movie documentary *Miliband of Brothers* (alongside his younger brother Ben) either side of shooting *The Inbetweeners* between 2008–10. Continuing on the comedy route in 2010, Henry featured in the hidden-camera show *Olivia Lee: Dirty, Sexy, Funny*, a show where Olivia Lee and other actors would set up comedic situations with the idea of unknowingly embarrassing the British public.

In 2011 Henry wrote and starred in his first TV short film *Colonel Gaddafi: The Lost Footage*, a comedy about the Libyan dictator who decides to flee to the West to take refuge but fails to settle in to western culture. Henry played the part of Muamar, alongside Charlie Creed-Miles as Trevor.

A year later Henry played the role of Burisov in the 2012 film *Anna Karenina*, alongside a wealth of acting royalty, including Keira Knightley, Jude Law, Matthew Macfadyen and Emily Watson. In 2014 he continued on the same path of mixing with this type of company, when he played the role of Charles Bovary in the film *Madame Bovary*, alongside Mia Wasikowska, Paul Giamatti and Rhys Ifans.

Twitter

As with many of our *Inbetweeners* stars, Henry is a prolific Twitter user and has tweeted over 7,000 times to his 2,150-odd followers. Henry tweets a lot about cricket (strange coming from a posh boy!). He is an avid Queens Park Rangers football supporter and, in general, shouts out to his friends and followers a lot. Here's a taste of what to expect when following @MatineeIdl:

'Leicester 2-0 down and Burnley 1-1… so far so good for the super hoops #QPR.' Results going the way of Henry's team.

'Everyone is brilliant in August: Osage County but Julianne Nicholson is out of this world.' Henry gives some respect to a fellow actor.

'No no no! One of the gods has gone! Philip Seymour Hoffman I salute you. RIP.' In remembrance of one of Henry's favourite actors, Philip Seymour Hoffman, who died in February 2014.

Emily Atack

Emily Atack made her name as the subject of desire of some of the characters from *The Inbetweeners*, playing the part of Charlotte Hinchcliffe in six episodes from 2008–10.

Background

Born in Luton, England, on 18 December 1989, Emily was part of an artistic family with a musician as a father and her mother being the actress Kate Robbins. Kate is most famous for appearing in the ITV drama *Crossroads* and for nine years she was a voiceover artist for the satirical comedy show *Spitting Image*. She has also played roles in many British comedy and drama series, such as *Dinnerladies*, *Last of the Summer Wine*, *Heartbeat*, *Where the Heart Is*, *Doctors* and *Casualty*. In addition, she also released a number of music singles between 1978 and 1988, with her biggest hit 'More Than In Love' reaching number two in the UK charts in 1981. A tough act to follow for Emily!

Career

Emily's first major role came when playing Kelly Lang in the ITV police drama *Blue Murder*. The show starred Caroline Quentin as DCI Janine Lewis from 2003–09. She would then go on to play the character of Cathy Dee in the long-running series *Heartbeat*, before landing the role of Charlotte Hinchcliffe in *The Inbetweeners*. Emily featured in the episodes 'The First Day', 'Girlfriend', 'Xmas Party', 'Work Experience', 'Will's Birthday' and 'The Fashion Show'.

It was after she finished *The Inbetweeners* that the UK went crazy for Emily and her alter-ego Charlotte; the lads' mags couldn't wait to obtain her as a cover girl and *FHM* snapped her up for a couple of raunchy shoots in 2010 and 2012.

Back to the acting, in 2010 Emily featured in the pilot for the BBC *Only Fools and Horses* spin-off *Rock & Chips*, alongside co-*Inbetweeners'* star James Buckley. In the pilot Emily played the part of Marion, a character who never featured in the full series of the show.

In 2013 Emily confirmed to *Digital Spy* that she would not be joining the other Inbetweeners in the sequel movie, stating: '*The Inbetweeners* is something I did quite a long time ago now. It was the most amazing thing ever and I wish them all the love and luck in the world but I just think time's gone on now.' Despite that, she still scored her first big-screen role in the British film *Get Lucky*, a movie about a small-time villain who gets mixed up in a criminal world beyond his imagination. Emily plays the part of Bridget in the film, which also stars Luke Treadaway, whose previous acting credits include *Attack the Block*, and *Clash of the Titans*; Craig Fairbrass, whose previous roles have included the 1993 movie *Cliffhanger*, *EastEnders* from 1999–2001 and a voice for the 2007 video game *Call of Duty: Modern Warfare*. After the film was made, Atack told *Red Carpet News TV* what she thought of the project: 'I like the fact that the characters are likeable. With a lot of British gangster films they can be very dark and shocking. With this [*Get Lucky*], there is also a comedy element.' Unfortunately, the critics certainly found there to be a comedy element in the film. Here is what they had to say:

'Luke Treadaway is miscast as a hardened criminal in this British gangster flick about a casino heist. There's the odd decent twist, but plot holes and stilted dialogue abound: hardly anyone swears in this alternative version of London's underworld.' Anna Smith, *Empireonline.com*.

'Though a superior addition to the ridiculously high quantity of London gangster comedy/dramas of recent years, *Get Lucky* is just about watchable and at times fun, but lacks the script or characters to elevate it from forgettable clichéd mediocrity.' *Burford's Big Bad Blog*.

Ouch! Well, besides what the critics think, we think anything with Emily Atack in deserves a watch!

In her personal life, Emily admitted in late 2013 that she dated One Direction star Harry Styles. However, it was very much seen as a bit of fun, as she told *Reveal* magazine: 'We were never boyfriend and girlfriend. I think that's the first time I've ever admitted to what it was because I've always just shrugged it off before. But I think it's best to clear it up. So, yeah, we had a short-lived thing that was just a bit of fun. Then we went off in our opposite directions.'

Twitter

Aside from acting, Emily is a massive social-media user. Her Twitter account has nearly 100,000 followers with over 6,000 tweets and her Instagram account has over 800 posts and nearly 20,000 followers – can't think why! That said, there's always a bit of banter flying around on the Twittersphere and photos aplenty on Instagram. Let's take a look at @EmAtack's tweet highlights:

'There's a grey goose waddling around in my head being a right prick. Thank you @AuraMayfair for a great night!' A nasty hangover after a birthday night out at a top London nightspot.

'Cracking up I called it Life of PIE! Seemed wrong writing Pi. It was good. Bit weird, but good. The lad playing Pi is a lad.

Love him.' Emily getting the name of the film badly wrong and a big shout out to Suraj Sharma.

'Just watched the first 3 episodes of Breaking Bad on Netflix. Why, in the name of god, have I never seen this before?' Agreed! How did it take Emily until May 2013 to find *Breaking Bad*?!

'Christ. I forgot The Snowman has a depressing ending. "If you've been affected by issues raised in this animation please call…"' Emily prepares for the worst at Christmas time!

Belinda Stewart-Wilson
Background
Belinda Stewart-Wilson, aka MILF Mrs Polly McKenzie in *The Inbetweeners*, was born on 16 April 1971 in London, England. Her father is Sir Blair Stewart-Wilson, who between 1976 and 1994 was one of Queen Elizabeth II's personal attendants, a role bestowed upon him after climbing the ranks of the military. In her youth, Belinda attended the Hurst Lodge School in Ascot, Berkshire, a school for children aged 3–18 that specialises in teaching performing arts and dance. Former pupils of the Hurst Lodge School include Sarah 'Fergie' Ferguson, the Duchess of York.

After completing school, Stewart-Wilson then trained at the Webber Douglas Academy of Dramatic Art, a drama school founded in 1926 in London. The school has many famous alumni, including Angela Lansbury, Hugh Bonneville, Minnie Driver and Terence Stamp.

Stewart-Wilson was married to actor and comedian Ben Miller. However, they divorced in 2011. They have one son together. Ben Miller is most famous for being one half of the comedy double-act Armstrong & Miller with Alexander

Armstrong. Along with *The Armstrong & Miller Show*, Miller has appeared in a plethora of British comedies, including *French & Saunders*, *The Catherine Tate Show*, *Paul Merton: The Series*, and alongside Rowan Atkinson in the film *Johnny English*. Aside from comedy, he is also famous for appearing in the ITV drama *Primeval* (starring alongside Belinda Stewart-Wilson) and most recently *Death in Paradise* as DI Richard Poole.

Career

Belinda's first major acting role was to play Dilys Perkins in the ITV series *Shine on Harvey Moon*. After that she would go on to play a number of roles in both comedy and drama. Here are some of her other highlights:

Agatha Christie's Poirot – Belinda played the part of the dubbing secretary in the episode 'Murder on the Links'. The long-running drama ran on ITV from 1989–2013 for a total of 70 episodes.

Goodnight Sweetheart – In 1996 Belinda played a minor role in the episode 'The Yanks are Coming'. The series saw Nicholas Lyndhurst time travel from the 1990s to the 1940s during World War II and consequently live a double life.

Holby City – This long-running hospital drama series first aired on BBC1 in 1999 and is still as popular today as it has ever been. The show takes its name from the original hospital that was part of the BBC series *Casualty*, which is also still running today and has been since 1986. Belinda played the part of Jo Wheeler in the episode 'Under Pressure' in 2004.

Broken News – The satirical news comedy made fun of 24-hour news programmes and ran on BBC2 in 2005. The show was created by John Morton, a satire connoisseur whose other writing credits include *Twenty Twelve*. Belinda played the character of Amanda Panda in the episodes 'Hijack', 'Half Way There Day' and 'Crime'.

Jekyll – A television series that featured James Nesbitt as a descendant of Dr Jekyll who begins to transform himself into a modern-day Mr Hyde. The show was written by Steven Moffat, a Scottish writer, producer and director who has written a number of *Doctor Who* episodes. Belinda Stewart-Wilson featured in episodes one and four, playing the part of Nicki.

The Peter Serafinowicz Show – Belinda played a number of different characters in this comedy-sketch show, which aired on BBC2 in 2007. Peter Serafinowicz, who created and wrote the show, is most famous for playing a major role in the zombie comedy film *Shaun of the Dead*.

Primeval – Belinda played the role of Christine Johnson in the third series of the science-fiction TV drama, alongside her then husband Ben Miller. *Primeval* was created by Adrian Hodges and Tim Haines, a pair who, together, have writing and directing credits for various TV shows and documentaries.

The IT Crowd – The comedy created by the brains behind *Father Ted*, Graham Linehan, was a huge success on Channel 4 and starred Chris O'Dowd and Richard Ayoade. Stewart-Wilson played the part of Victoria Reynholm, wife of Douglas Reynholm.

The Impressions Show with Culshaw and Stephenson – Utilising her impressionist skills, Belinda played the part of a sultry and seductive Nigella Lawson in three episodes in series two in 2010.

Ripper Street – The BBC drama ran over two series in 2012 and 2013 and takes place in London six months after the infamous Jack the Ripper murders. The show ran for 16 episodes in total and Belinda features in the fifth episode of the second series, named 'Threads of Silk and Gold'.

Along with these major roles, Belinda has also played smaller parts in various comedies, such as *My Family*, *Little Crackers* and *Citizen Khan*.

After playing Will's fit mum in *The Inbetweeners*, the world went crazy for Polly McKenzie, so much so that Belinda made a saucy shoot for *FHM* in 2011. The lads' mag also did an interview in which she spoke about what it's like to be a pin-up MILF!

> I think with *The Inbetweeners* it's all in the boys' imaginations; they're so rude about her. She's not really a prostitute or a stripper but in their heads she's all of those things. She's become incredibly popular by doing very little. I went to the read-through for the third series and I was literally blushing all the way through from what they were saying about me. It's filthy but that's why it's popular.

She also spoke about what she was like growing up, which seems a world away from the MILF we know and love today:

> I was never very good looking – I had my jaw pulled forward, I had a squint and a patch over one eye to straighten it up – so I thought I'd make people laugh to get them on my side. I thought it was quite cool though, as I was sure I looked like a pirate.

No matter what she says, we think she'll always be the ultimate MILF! Bad news though, lads, it seems that she won't be doing any more sexy shoots in the future. In an interview with Scotland's *Daily Record* in 2011, Belinda declared that now she has passed 40 years old it's probably about time to concentrate on the acting career – such a shame!

Although she has enjoyed playing the part of Polly McKenzie, Belinda told the *Mirror* after the third series that she now hopes to move on and find some other roles in the future. 'You strive for that for years and suddenly that role defines you for a while. It has been a great year but I do hope that at some stage in the future I might be seen as something else as well.'

Martin Trenaman

Background

Martin Trenaman is a British actor and writer born in 1965. He is best known in *Inbetweeners'* circles as playing Simon's dad, Alan Cooper, in the show. Aside from *The Inbetweeners*, he is well known on the comedy circuit as being a writer and has writing credits for many modern-day comedy programmes. As Martin has many credits to his name, we thought we would analyse both his acting and writing careers to give you a flavour of the influence Martin has on British comedy.

Career – Martin Trenaman, the Actor

Martin's first real acting break came when he appeared in the Channel 4 sketch-show series *Barking* in 1998. The show featured a whole host of rising stars at the time, including Mackenzie Crook, David Walliams, Omid Djalili, Peter Kay and Catherine Tate. It only lasted for one series but would be the springboard for many up-and-coming British comedians.

In 2000 Martin then went on to play the role of Mike Waters in the TV show *Hope and Glory*, a BBC television drama about a comprehensive school, which starred Lenny Henry. That same year Trenaman would stay with Lenny Henry to feature in his sketch-show comedy *Lenny Henry in Pieces*.

In 2001 Martin featured in the critically acclaimed Channel 4 comedy *Spaced*, which was written by and starred Jessica Stevenson and Simon Pegg. The show ran for two series between 1999 and 2001, and Martin played the character of Derek in the second episode of the second series, named 'Change'.

Randomly, Martin played a character in the daytime drama series *Dream Team*, a show about a fictional football team 'Harchester United' and the trials and tribulations of its players and their wives; Martin took the role of Mr McCoy in the episode 'Hit and Run' in 2003. We've all got to pay the bills somehow, Martin!

In 2004 he played a small part in the weird and wonderful sitcom *The Mighty Boosh*, which was created by and starred comedians Julian Barratt and Noel Fielding. Martin played the part of a locksmith in the episode 'Jungle' in 2004.

In the lead-up to playing Alan Cooper in *The Inbetweeners*, Martin played a number of small roles in comedy and drama programmes, including *Wire in the Blood*, an ITV crime drama starring Robson Green; *Saxondale*, the comedy written by Steve Coogan, who plays his character Tommy Saxondale; and *The Impressions Show with Culshaw and Stephenson* – where Martin would play himself in two episodes of the first series.

Since *The Inbetweeners* Martin has gone on to play a number of comedy roles, including *It's Kevin*, a comedy sketch-show series written by Kevin Eldon; *I Give it a Year*, the rom-com film starring Rose Byrne, Anna Farris, Stephen Merchant and Minnie Driver; and *Babylon*, the police drama/comedy directed by Danny Boyle. However, probably the most successful project that Martin Trenaman undertook after *The Inbetweeners* was the E4 sitcom *PhoneShop*, which focuses on the career of a graduate, Christopher, who subsequently gains employment. Martin plays the store manager of a fictional mobile-phone shop in London.

Career – Martin Trenaman, the Writer

You may not know it but Martin has had a hand in many British comedies since the mid to late 1990s, just not always as an actor. Let's take a look at his work over the years.

Starting in 1995, Martin would write additional material for stand-up comedy DVDs, including *Lee Evans: Live from the West End*, *Peter Kay Feels...* and *Is it Bill Bailey?*

Perhaps Martin's big break came in 2002 when he co-created and wrote a number of episodes for the TV sitcom *15 Storeys High*. The show takes place in a tower block in London with two main characters: Vince Clarke, who is played by Sean Lock, and Errol Spears, played by Benedict Wong. The sitcom received a very positive reaction from the press, with many newspaper critics comparing it to *Seinfeld* and calling it the best show on television at the time.

After tasting life in front of the camera in the early- to mid-2000s, Martin reverted back to being a writer, when in 2006 he rekindled his comedy relationship with Sean Lock and started to write episodes for the Channel 4 talk show *TV Heaven, Telly Hell*, where guests would come on and speak to Lock about their likes and dislikes on television; not too dissimilar to the BBC show *Room 101*. In an interview with *Digital Spy* in 2011, Martin told us his own idea of TV heaven and telly hell:

> It's probably going to be *Seinfeld* — that's one of my favourites. Although I like *Family Guy* as well — I'm a big fan of that... But there's loads that I'd just put the boot through the telly! *Antiques Roadshow* — Christ! How is that still being made? It's absolutely astonishing. There [are] various others — some of those BBC1 comedy dramas that they think are funny. Oh my God! But I shouldn't slag them off too much, I might get a part in one!

Trenaman continued to write comedy material throughout his time playing Alan Cooper in *The Inbetweeners*. Some of his writing credits include *The Big Fat Quiz of the Year*, an annual comedy panel show looking at the events of the year gone by; *Argumental*, a comedy panel show where two captains and their guests debate various topics; and *A Comedy Roast*, in which Martin wrote additional material for the episodes featuring Bruce Forsyth, Chris Tarrant and Barbara Windsor.

In 2011–12 Martin wrote additional material for the Channel 4 stand-up comedy show *Stand Up For The Week*, a programme where comedians would run through a stand-up routine on a particular topic or carry out tasks specified by the host. Regular guests of the show, which has been running since 2010, are Seann Walsh, Josh Widdicombe, Rich Hall, Jon Richardson, Jack Whitehall and Kevin Bridges.

Martin's most notable writing credit spanned over nine years between 2003–2012, when he wrote additional material for the BBC2 comedy panel show *Never Mind the Buzzcocks*. The programme took on the premise of two team captains who were joined by guests to answer questions and carry out tasks to a music theme. The show has been running since 1996 and has seen a number of hosts, captains and guests over the years, including Mark Lamarr, Simon Amstell, Phil Jupitus, Sean Hughes, Bill Bailey and Noel Fielding. Martin Trenaman has written additional material for 112 episodes. It has, to date, been running for 27 series, with 256 episodes.

Robin Weaver
Background
Probably one of the most experienced actors in *The Inbetweeners*, Robin Weaver plays the part of Simon's mum, Pamela Cooper, for nine episodes, those being 'The First Day', 'Bunk Off', 'Thorpe Park', 'Will's Birthday', 'The Duke of Edinburgh Awards', 'Exam Time', 'The Fashion Show', 'Trip to Warwick' and 'Camping Trip'. As Mrs Cooper, not only is she the bane of Simon's life through high school but she also has to go through the trials and tribulations of her own marriage – not that Simon has any empathy!

Career
Robin has appeared in many TV shows and films since she got her first major acting role in 1989 in a TV movie named *Somewhere to Run*. After that she gained another big role in the Jim Henson 1992 production *A Muppet Christmas Carol*, playing the part of Clara.

It was between 1992 and 1994 that Robin would appear in her first comedy TV series, when she played the character of Jade Carver in the BBC1 show *Love Hurts*. The show centred around the character of Tessa (played by Zoe Wanamaker) who finds herself going through a difficult break-up but finds love again in the arms of Frank (played by Adam Faith).

While Robin would play other drama roles continuing into the 1990s, it was in comedy where she started to find her feet, and from 2004 she found herself playing roles in series such as *The Lenny Henry Show*, *The Catherine Tate Show*, *Broken News*, *Green Wing* and *My Family*, before gaining the part of Pamela Cooper in *The Inbetweeners* in 2008.

After *The Inbetweeners* Robin picked up some small parts in the long-running BBC medical drama *Doctors*, a cameo in the award-winning satirical comedy *Twenty Twelve* and a recurring role in *Casualty*. Her most recent work came in 2012, when she featured in the British Sky 1 sitcom *Trollied* and the BBC show *Him & Her*.

Trollied follows the workers at a fictional supermarket in Warrington called Valco and stars Jane Horrocks (a British actress most famous for her roles in *Absolutely Fabulous*, *Corpse Bride* and *Chicken Run*) and Joel Fry (of *White Van Man*, *Twenty Twelve*, *Plebs* and *Game of Thrones*). After the first series in 2011, Sky 1 announced that they would commission a further two series of the show in 2012 and 2013, each 13 episodes long. After the third series, it was still to be decided if *Trollied* would receive a fourth run. However, Jane Horrocks announced that she would be leaving the sitcom in December 2013. Let's take a look at what the critics made of *Trollied*.

'I have to say I laughed all the way through and found the material between Gavin and Julie to be rather touching. Whether the show can survive without Jane Horrocks remains to be seen, but I did feel she got a fitting and respectful send-off in this rather good Christmas Special.' Matt Donnelly, *The Custard TV*.

'Giggles are few and far between down at Valco, which is a shame because with such a strong cast the supermarket sitcom should offer much better value.' Hannah Verdier, *The Guardian*.

'*Trollied* is not so much "every little helps"; but a little tends to go a long way. Supermarket sitcom *Trollied* had a mixed reception for its first series: the script was undeniably appalling but a few critics were clearly charmed by characters and scenarios that were bold, obvious and easy on the brain.' Sharon Lougher, *Metro*.

After *Trollied*, Robin made an appearance in the BBC3 sitcom *Him & Her*. She played the character of The Registrar in the final series, which saw the two main characters get married.

John Seaward

There have to be some geeks in Rudge Park Comprehensive and, luckily for *The Inbetweeners*, there was Big John, played by John Seaward.

Background

John was born in London on 22 August 22 1988 and, before he appeared in *The Inbetweeners*, his first minor acting role came in the BBC sitcom *Lead Balloon*, created and written by Jack Dee and Pete Sinclair. The show depicts Jack Dee's character Rick as a cynical comedian who is plagued by petty annoyances, not too dissimilar to Larry David's character in the American sitcom *Curb Your Enthusiasm*. Receiving mixed reviews from the critics, *Lead Balloon* ran for four series from 2006–11 and John played the character of an Awards Guest in the third episode of the first series.

Career

In 2008 John found himself playing the character of Luke in an episode of the BBC science-fiction drama *Survivors*, which ran from 2008–10. The premise of the programme was a group of people who had survived a deathly and rare type of influenza. The show was created by Adrian Hodges (best known for ITV drama *Primeval* and writing the screenplay for the 2011 film *My Week with Marylin*) and is based on the TV series and novel *Survivors*, written by Terry Nation. John featured in the fourth episode of the first of two series.

Other TV Work

After appearing in *The Inbetweeners* and *The Inbetweeners Movie*, John appeared in a short film called *Future.Inc*, directed by Martin Stirling and written by Andrew Ellard, a writer, producer and director who has worked on a number of British TV shows, such as *Red Dwarf* and *The IT Crowd*. *Future.Inc* focused on the life of a 20-something girl working in a mundane job who finds a new social-media network that could change her life, but would turn out to have devastating consequences.

David Schaal

We know him as the foul-mouthed Terry Cartwright, also familiar as Jay's dad from *The Inbetweeners*, but what do we know about the actor David Schaal? Along with Robin Weaver and Martin Trenaman, David is one of the more seasoned cast members and has plied his trade across a number of British TV shows since the early 1990s.

Background

David was born on 27 May 1963 in London and from 1985–88 he studied Theatre Arts at the Rose Bruford College of Speech and Drama (now known as the Rose Bruford College of Theatre & Performance), a school in Kent that offers degrees in many categories and has some notable alumni in Tom Baker and none other than legendary actor Gary Oldman.

Career

After his education, he then started to make a name for himself as an actor. Let's take a look at some of his acting highlights before playing the great Mr Terry Cartwright.

London's Burning – The popular ITV drama ran from 1988–2002 and is where David made his acting debut as a security guard in series two, episode one.

Our Friends in the North – In 1996 David appeared in the BBC drama following four friends from the north-east of England, which starred Christopher Eccleston and Daniel Craig. He played a part as a prison officer in the episode depicting *1984*.

Grange Hill – David played the part of Tom Hargreaves in this long-running BBC drama series. The show, which ran from 1978–2008, has featured many soap actors that we know and love today and was made famous for its gritty and honest storylines that many teenagers could relate to. David was in the show for 11 episodes in total in 2000 and 2001.

The Armando Iannucci Shows – In 2001 writer and director Armando Iannucci produced a series of shows on Channel 4 that featured sketches and commentary regarding his views on human nature and existentialism. David featured as characters in four out of the eight episodes that were made.

The Office – Quite similar to the role he played in *The Inbetweeners*, David played the foul-mouthed and crude character of Glynn, or 'Taffy' as he was known to David Brent. The mockumentary followed the life of Ricky Gervais and Stephen Merchant character Brent trying to run a paper merchandising company in the sleepy town of Slough. *The Office* went on to win numerous awards during the time it was on air between 2001 and 2003.

The IT Crowd – David starred as Dec in the episode 'The Work Outing' of the comedy series, which follows two IT professionals (Chris O'Dowd and Richard Ayoade) and their hapless endeavours in life and the workplace.

Ashes-to-Ashes – Sequel to the BBC drama *Life on Mars*, *Ashes-to-Ashes* revolved around the story of a policewoman in 2008 who is shot and finds herself in the year 1981. The show stars Keeley Hawes and Philip Glenister as the London detectives. Schaal featured as Gene's (Glenister's) lookalike in episode seven.

The Inbetweeners – David played Terry Cartwright for five episodes in the show, in a role where he set out to humiliate his son Jay in front of his friends. The episodes he appeared in were 'Caravan Club', 'Work Experience', 'Exam Time', 'The Gig and the Girlfriend' and 'Will is Home Alone'.

In the lead-up to playing Terry Cartwright, David took a number of roles in British TV shows, such as *Peak Practice*, *Silent Witness*, *Hustle*, *Doc Martin*, *Kidulthood*, *EastEnders*, *The Bill* and *Casualty*.

Other TV Work
Since *The Inbetweeners* and *The Inbetweeners Movie*, David Schaal has continued his acting and writing career by featuring in

popular TV shows *White Van Man* and Jack Dee's sitcom *Lead Balloon*. Most recently he has played a small role in the Channel 4 soap opera *Hollyoaks* – it's a pretty safe bet that the colourful language associated with some of his better-known characters would be absent in his latest role.

Additionally, Schaal has written a number of short films and plays, along with directing various productions at the Edinburgh Festival in 2010, and in 2012 he wrote and directed the play *Brotherly Love* for The Real London Ensemble, a story about two brothers' fight with addiction and class. David told *edfestmag.com* about the play: 'It's really about addiction and what happens when addiction hits families and how it disintegrates. It's actually a black comedy even though it's a serious subject matter.'

Dominic Applewhite

Otherwise known as Simon's annoying little brother Andrew Cooper in *The Inbetweeners*, Dominic Applewhite has enjoyed a fantastic career so far and, at only 19 years of age, it looks like he's got a great future ahead of him.

Background

Andrew grew up in the small town of Princes Risborough in Buckinghamshire, a town just under 10 miles south of Aylesbury in the south-east of England. Before gaining the role as Andrew Cooper, Dominic's first acting job was playing the part of Billy Snodgrass in the BBC children's sci-fi adventure series *M.I. High* in 2008. During that same year, writers Damon Beesley and Iain Morris offered Dominic the part of Andrew in *The Inbetweeners*.

Career

It was after *The Inbetweeners* when things really took off for Dominic. At the age of 14 he played the part of Valentine Logue in the award-winning film *The King's Speech*, alongside Colin Firth, Helena Bonham Carter and Geoffrey Rush, among a raft of other stars. Dominic's character in the film was that of the son of the King's speech therapist Lionel Logue. In 2011 the film won a plethora of awards, including four Oscars (Best Motion Picture, Best Actor, Best Director, Best Writing in an Original Screenplay) and three BAFTAs (Best British Film, Anthony Asquith Award for Film Music, Best Film).

Dominic's next role was in the CBBC drama *Postcode* in 2011. The series was a gritty drama aimed at bridging the class, ethnicity and gang divide in the suburbs of London, in the same way that similar BBC shows in the past, such as *Byker Grove* and *Grange Hill*, have tried to do. *The Guardian* describes *Postcode* and also gives an insight into the challenges while filming:

> The filming started in Stockwell, south London, the day after the August riots erupted. It feels edgy – in one scene the fictional gang members gatecrash a party by climbing over the garden wall. The producer, Elaine Sperber, said the crew who were filming only just managed to prevent having one of their cameras from being stolen.

Dominic played the part of Freddie in the first three episodes of the show.

A year later in 2012, Dominic played various roles in the comedy-sketch show *Watson & Oliver*, devised and written by Lorna Watson and Ingrid Oliver. The pair were first discovered at the Edinburgh Fringe Festival before their show was picked up by BBC2 for two seasons during 2012–13. The show revolved around Watson and Oliver making fun of various current TV shows, such as *Made in Chelsea* and *Call the Midwife*, and portraying popular culture in general. It received mixed reception from the critics. Here's what some of them had to say:

'Three episodes into its second series, *Watson & Oliver* is actually not bad and is often quite clever and subversive for a mainstream comedy, but it could definitely be improved.' Bruce Dessau, *Beyond the Joke*.

'Watson & Oliver are obviously very talented comedy performers and writers, having three sell-out Edinburgh shows under their belts, and the supporting cast, though fairly sparse, also offer strong performances. It's not going to break any boundaries or change the way you think, but if you are looking for an entertaining and varied half hour then do give it a go.' Shaun Spencer, *Giggle Beats*.

'Does mainstream necessarily have to mean poor? As something like *Miranda* has shown us, absolutely not. However, *Watson & Oliver*, the sketch show from Lorna Watson and Ingrid Oliver, is the counter-argument.' John Robinson, *The Guardian*.

Sightseers was the next project that Dominic undertook in 2012. He played the part of a blond teenager in the black comedy starring Alice Lowe and Steve Oram about the tribulations of a couple who take a caravan holiday. The British film was produced by Edgar Wright, who is most famous for working on the Simon Pegg and Nick Frost films *Shaun of the Dead*, *Hot Fuzz* and *The World's End*.

2012 was topped off for Dominic with a part in the all-star film production of *Les Misérables*, where he appeared alongside acting greatness in the form of Hugh Jackman, Russell Crowe, Anna Hathaway and Helena Bonham Carter. In February 2013 the film won numerous awards, including three Oscars (Best Supporting Actress, Best Makeup and Hairstyling and Best Sound Mixing), and four BAFTAs (Best Supporting Actress, Best Makeup and Hair, Best Sound and Best Production Design). Despite the array of awards and honours, *Les Misérables* received a range of reviews from the critics, ranging from the good, the bad and the indifferent. Interestingly, the British press, such as *The Guardian* and *The Daily Telegraph*, gave the film rave reviews. However, across the pond the reviews were hit and miss. *The Hollywood Reporter* and *The New York Times* both gave the film kudos for its effects and cinematography but both said it left a little to be desired in terms of the plot and audience engagement.

Back to Dominic, and what a credit list already for such a young actor. And his achievements haven't stopped there. In August 2013 he got two A★ and an A in his A-Level exams. After receiving the results, Dominic told the *Bucks Herald* about how he managed to juggle his studies and acting:

I'm delighted. I knew quite early on in the school year I was going to be doing *Les Misérables* so I was able to timetable things and juggle exam revision and filming.

Les Misérables was pretty intensive last year. Luckily I only missed a few days off school. I've always been pretty academic minded as much as the performing arts side of things but it is what I want to do as a profession.

I like keeping myself busy. I'm one of those who works really well under pressure. It got pretty crazy last year and

I was able to hold it together. Perhaps it made me work even harder.

After achieving such fantastic results in his exams, Dominic is currently studying music at New College, Oxford University. New College is currently ranked highest for the performance of its scholars and is one of the oldest and most prestigious establishments in the world since its inception in 1379. The college also has an impressive list of alumni, ranging from actors to politicians and academics, such as Kate Beckinsale, Angus Deayton and Tony Benn.

Twitter

Along with his studies and acting, Dominic also makes use of the social-media network Twitter to engage with his 435 followers. He's got some way to go to reach Blake Harrison's level on Twitter but let's see what he's had to say for himself since he joined the 'Twitteratti' in 2012:

'My mum asked if I wanted to help cook dinner. See, I would, but I'm scared there might be a #flashinthepan.' Luckily, the writers of *The Inbetweeners* can come up with better lines than that!

'@russellcrowe A huge thanks once again for a fantastic evening. It was a real pleasure to meet you! All the best.' Dominic does a bit of namedropping and thanks a fellow cast member for his '*Les Mis*' party.

'While a baby crying is the most stressful sound, I think a baby's laugh is the most beautiful sound in the world.' A little bit of philosophy goes a long way on Twitter!

'I could wake up tomorrow and Mitt Romney could be the

US President. And then hopefully I'll wake up again after a horrible nightmare.' It's a shame he isn't taking politics at Oxford! Dominic chats through the US election in 2012.

'Sitting next to a bunch of primary-age kids singing Miley Cyrus songs. Caught between cute and depressing.' Dominic tweets about the finer points of popular music.

Alex MacQueen
Background

Alex MacQueen plays the character of Neil's 'gay' dad Kevin Sutherland in *The Inbetweeners*. Alex was born in Epsom, Surrey in 1974 and was educated at the St John's School in Leatherhead, an independent school for pupils aged 13–18. After his secondary school education, he studied English at Durham University and received a first and then went on to study for a Master of Philosophy at Pembroke College, Cambridge University.

During the years of 1992–95 Alex was a member of the National Youth Theatre, a charity in London dedicated to developing young people through creativity. Since it was founded in 1956, the National Youth Theatre has been a breeding ground for some of the UK's most talented actors and actresses, including Daniel Day-Lewis, Dame Helen Mirren, Daniel Craig, Ben Kingsley, Colin Firth and Orlando Bloom. Throughout the years the theatre has produced many high-profile productions and in 2012 members of the theatre performed for the Olympic and Paralympic teams as they entered the Olympic Village.

Career

After finishing university, Alex wouldn't go straight into acting – quite the contrary, in fact. He trained as a barrister after graduating in 1998 and found himself working as a Business Affairs Executive for Granada International, which is now known as ITV Studios and based in Manchester and London. Alex then worked in the House of Commons with members of the Culture and Media Select Committee. MacQueen told *British Comedy Guide* about his decision to move away from law:

> I thought to myself, 'I just can't do this, this isn't what I want to be doing,' so I left that world. Very fortunately, I bumped into a casting director called Lucy Bevan in a theatre foyer and she asked what I was up to, and I said I wanted to become an actor. She told me she was casting for a film the following week and suggested I read for one of the parts.

It would be in 2003 that Alex started his acting career, appearing in the TV series *Keen Eddie*, a comedy that starred Sienna Miller and Alexei Sayle. Alex appeared in the episode 'Eddie Loves Baseball'. After a few small roles in British TV, Alex gained a part in the film *Keeping Mum* in 2005. The film was a black comedy starring Rowan Atkinson, Kristin Scott Thomas, Maggie Smith and Patrick Swayze. Alex played the part of a train-ticket collector in the film, which collected mixed reviews from the critics.

After gaining experience in the conventional acting world, Alex then started to turn his hand to comedy and in 2005 he played a short role in the critically acclaimed comedy series *Peep*

Show, starring David Mitchell and Robert Webb. The series was well received by the critics due to its original style and the way it was shot (consistently through the viewpoint of the characters). Alex played the part of the jury foreman in the episode 'Jurying'.

That very same year Alex gained his biggest role to date as Dr Keith Greene in the BBC series *Holby City* and, during the years 2005–2010, he starred in 75 episodes as the consultant anaesthetist, who also featured in *Holby's* sister-series *Casualty* for one episode in 2006. Throughout his time playing doctors and nurses, he kept up his comedy roles and made appearances in a number of British TV sitcoms, including *The IT Crowd*, *Pulling*, *Lead Balloon*, *The Thick of it*, *Outnumbered*, *Miranda*, *The Increasingly Poor Decisions of Todd Margaret*, and, of course, from 2008–10, *The Inbetweeners*.

Throughout the series, Neil's dad is very much the butt of jokes about being very camp and is often referred to as a 'bender', to Neil's constant denial. Kevin Sutherland is very much a part of the episode 'Bunk Off', when Simon and Will accuse him of touching them!

MacQueen's next major role after *The Inbetweeners* was *Hunderby*, a sitcom produced by Sky and broadcast on Sky Atlantic in 2012. The black comedy set in the 1830s was written by Julia Davies (of *Nighty Night* fame) and starred Alex as the character Edmund, a local vicar who courts Helene, a woman who is washed ashore after she becomes shipwrecked off the English coast. In 2012 the show won the awards for Best Sitcom and Best New Comedy Programme at the British Comedy Awards. Let's take a look at what the reviews had to say about *Hunderby*:

OTHER CAST & CREW MEMBERS

'Julia Davis and co-writer Barunka O'Shaughnessy must take several bows to deafening applause for this comic masterpiece. The hoot-per-minute rate has remained high throughout and among an exemplary cast, Alex MacQueen (as Edmund) did a full Sheryl Crow, moving from comedy backing singer to lead vocals with aplomb.' Julia Raeside, *The Guardian*.

'*Hunderby*, starring and written by Julia Davis is a fruity romp, and it benefited hugely from a comedy performer normally the butt of jibes seizing his chance of a lead role. Alex MacQueen – the biscuit-nibbling, blue-sky-thinking buffoon in *The Thick Of It*.' Aiden Smith, *The Scotsman*.

'There's heavy investment in an impeccable cast and setting, but I'm not sure what *Hunderby* is. Davis's reputation is for visiting icky places nobody else will brave; this is mainly innuendo and goofing, with gaps between gags as the linear story chugs on.' Jack Seale, *Radio Times*.

Other TV/Film Work

In 2013 Alex made his way onto the big screen, appearing in the films *I Give it a Year*, alongside fellow comedy actor Stephen Merchant, and feature film *Jack the Giant Slayer*, which starred Ewan McGregor and Ian McShane. Throughout the years, Alex has played a number of different roles and he told the *British Comedy Guide* about how comedy acting has become a natural progression:

I suppose, if I'm honest, I thought, 'oh, I'll just take whatever comes my way.' It turns out that comedy is what I've sort of done more of... but I do still enjoy doing 'normal acting', as it were too. However, the comedy just seems to have worked in a more permanent way, so that's what I'm doing. Most of the comedy I've been involved with is not really stand-up or slapstick or anything like that, it's quite naturalistic acting in a way.

In the same interview, he also tells us about getting recognised on the street:

I do get quite a few people recognising me from *The Inbetweeners* though. That's got quite a young fan base, and it's often young people who are interested in autographs and things like that, so that's definitely one of the sources the attention comes from at the moment. It's actually only a small role I have in *The Inbetweeners*, but people still recognise me.

Victoria Willing
Background
Victoria Willing was born in London in 1960 and is the daughter of Dame Paula Rego, a Portuguese-born award-winning artist.

Victoria plays the role of Mrs Cartwright (Jay's Mum) in *The Inbetweeners*. She appears in three episodes of the show, from 2008–10, which were 'Caravan Club', 'Will's Birthday' and 'Will is Home Alone'. After starting her acting career in 1990, Victoria made a name for herself as a muppet, quite literally! She played a voice of a muppet in the films *The Muppet Christmas Carol* and *Muppet Treasure Island*.

Career

During the early part of her career Victoria started to make a name for herself with small parts in successful British TV shows throughout the 1990s and early 2000s, such as *Pie in the Sky*, *Bramwell* and *The Knock*. Since 2000, Victoria has played several roles in a number of different shows in the UK and has played one-off and recurring characters in shows like *The Bill*, *Holby City*, *Casualty*, *Doctors*, *Wire in the Blood*, *Silent Witness* and, of course, *The Inbetweeners* and *The Inbetweeners Movie*.

Along with her acting work, Victoria has also played a part behind the camera too. She worked as a puppeteer on the 1999 TV movie *Alice in Wonderland* (a film that starred Gene Wilder, Whoopi Goldberg and Ken Dodd!) and also as a puppeteer in the children's TV show *Bunnytown*.

Kacey Barnfield

Background

Kacey Barnfield plays the part of Neil's incredibly 'fit sister' Katie Sutherland in *The Inbetweeners*. She was born in Hackney, London on 14 January 14 1988 and has played a number of film and TV roles since she burst onto the scene in 2001. At one time she was dating England international cricketer Stuart Broad. However, the relationship appears to have subsided due to Kacey moving to Los Angeles in January 2011, presumably to pursue her career on the big screen.

Career

Kacey's first major acting role was playing the part of Maddie Gilks in the children's drama series *Grange Hill*. Throughout the time the show was on air between 1978 and 2008, the high-school drama looked to break boundaries and deal with issues that are prominent with its youthful audience, such as drug addiction, knife crime, suicide and sexual abuse, to name a few. Kacey appeared in 82 episodes in total between 2001 and 2005.

After finishing *Grange Hill*, Kacey was 17 and looking to continue establishing herself in British TV and she would do just that by gaining roles in *The Bill* and *Casualty*, but it would be in 2010, after *The Inbetweeners*, when she would really start to gain momentum as an actress.

Kacey's first 'big screen' role was in the TV-film *Lake Placid 3*, a horror film about the creatures in Black Lane, Aroosstook County, Maine. Kacey played the part of Ellie in the film, which was not well received by the critics. It seems as if the only good-looking thing in the film was Kacey herself!

Fear not, Kacey, you would soon be back on the big screen, this time in the big-budget film *Resident Evil: Afterlife*, as the character Crystal Waters. The 3D film is the fourth in the *Resident Evil* film series based on the computer game of the same name. The movie stars the likes of Milla Jovovich and Wentworth Miller as characters searching for remaining survivors after a deadly 't-virus' outbreak. Overall, the film made around $296 million at the box office but received mixed reviews from the critics. The review site *Rotten Tomatoes* gave the film 23 per cent and *Empire Online* gave the film two out of five stars, suggesting, 'What fun there is to be had is undermined by drab 3D, hacked-out dialogue and rehashed plots.' Never mind the reviews, here's what Kacey said about working on the project when talking to *horror-asylum.com*:

I learned a lot, I worked with some very successful actors who were also great people and gave me sound advice. The movie was of a huge scale and so very impressive but it was still a job you know, mornings are early and days are long, it's not glitz and glamour. Milla Jovovich was wonderful and I admired how hard she works for such a physically demanding role. It is clear she is just so utterly dedicated. As successful as she is, she has no diva-like airs and graces, she is all about the job and her passion is so evident. Her, Wentworth Miller and I spent two whole days filming those underwater scenes together. Oh yeah, I also learned never spend two days under water without wearing ear plugs…

The following year, in 2011, Kacey played a leading role in the TV film *Jabberwock*. She plays the part of Anabel who, with her accomplices, has to save the village from a medieval creature. As the creature was computer generated, Kacey told *roguecinema.com* about working with a make-believe monster:

Well, I've worked on quite a few films that used CGI, and it isn't that hard. I mean it's a little strange sometimes, but you just have to use your imagination for it. So when you're running for your life from the monster, you just have to see it in your head and know that it's there chasing you.

It is interesting though because the image you get in your head when you're making the film is very different from the one that the tech guys put together in the finished film. A lot of times, unless we have an advanced showing or get to see a rough cut, we don't get to see the monster any sooner than the audience when the film premieres.

In 2013 Kacey continued down the horror and sci-fi movie road by playing leading roles in the films *Neron* and *I Spit on your Grave 2*. However, she did also manage to find time to play the part of Molly in the football hooliganism film *Green Street 3: Never Back Down*.

Along with acting, Kacey is also a model and has appeared in a number of lads' mags over the years, probably down to the scantily clad appearance she made in *The Inbetweeners* on the doorstep of Neil's house!

Twitter

As with many of our stars, she is also a major Twitter user and has just under 7,000 followers. Let's see what @kaceylbarnfield has been chatting about in the 'twittersphere':

'I'm nearly 25. Twenty bloody five. Who wants to be my "If we're single by the time we're 30" buddy…' Incredibly, no lads responded to Kacey's request back in December 2012!

'Pretty impressed that I've been riding a bike with no brakes for the past few days and I haven't died yet. :)' Kacey gives her followers a scare by announcing she is also a stunt woman!

'Happy 35th Anniversary Grange Hill – Forever proud to be a small part of your legacy! X' A tribute to *Grange Hill*, one of Kacey's first acting roles.

'When Americans find out you're English they often like to put on their (worst) English accent and say "Ooooh, do you like tea and crumpets?"' Kacey on the culture difference between the UK and America.

'Django Unchained. (I'm slow on the uptake with this one). But how brilliant is it. Tarantino genius.' On viewing Tarantino's most recent film.

Waen Shepherd

Background

Waen Shepherd is an English actor, writer and composer, who played the part of Mr 'Paedo' Kennedy in the second series of *The Inbetweeners*. He was born in Yorkshire, England in 1971 and graduated from Oxford University in 1993 with a degree in Philosophy and Psychology.

Waen is probably best known for playing the character of Gary Le Strange, an eccentric but deluded cult-rock and new-romantic music performer. The performances of Le Strange have earned Waen cult status and his alter-ego still performs concerts and releases music to his niche fan base. After announcing the character at the Edinburgh Fringe, he went on to receive the Perrier Award for Best Newcomer in 2003. Shepherd would then introduce Gary Le Strange to the small screen in 2007 as part of ITV2's series *Comedy Cuts*. After playing the character for so long, Waen described to *thevelvetonion.com* how he found it hard to develop Gary Le Strange:

> The main thing in my head was that it worked, so I should do it again. But I got so much other work out of it that it became harder to devote time to creating it. Plus, the more people are watching you, the harder it is to experiment, and I instantly found that new songs wouldn't go down as well, because they just weren't ready yet. That was a hard lesson to learn.

Career

Waen's first major TV role came in 2006 when he played the part of Captain Helix in the British sci-fi comedy *Hyperdrive*, a show created by comedy writers Kevin Cecil and Andy Riley and starring comedians Nick Frost, Kevin Eldon and Miranda Hart. The show ran for two series with a total of twelve episodes and Waen featured in seven of them.

A year later, in 2007, Waen appeared in the short comedy film *World of Wrestling*, a spoof film about the lives of British wrestlers from the past who have to make it home safely after a night out on the town! Although dubbed as a short film, the piece contained a raft of comedy talent, including Mackenzie Crook, Kris Marshall, Kevin Eldon and Miranda Hart.

In 2009 Waen appeared in an episode of the BBC3 sitcom *We Are Klang*, a show devised by the comedy trio that featured Waen's co-star in *The Inbetweeners* Greg Davies. Waen appears as The Juggler in the episode 'Crime'.

In 2013 Waen rekindled his love for music and comedy when he starred in, and composed the music for, 10 episodes of the TV mini-series *The Day They Came to Suck Out Our Brains!* The spoof zombie series featured Warwick Davies, among other comedy actors. Waen featured in the episode 'The Wrath of Ken'.

Count Arthur Strong was the next project Waen undertook. The show (originally *Count Arthur Strong's Radio Show* broadcast on BBC Radio 4) was created by Steve Delaney and Graham Linehan and revolves around the story of Arthur Strong, an eccentric, semi-retired and out-of-work actor and his meeting with the son of his former comedy partner. The show ran for a series in July and August and was commissioned again for another series, much to the delight of the critics and those who enjoyed the original radio show. Waen appeared in the episode 'Athur.com', which originally aired on 15 July 2013.

Jonny Sweet

Background

Born in 1985, Jonny Sweet is the writing partner of Simon Bird and Joe Thomas. Jonny is most famous for being connected with the two Inbetweeners. However, he has carved out a career of his own since meeting the guys at Cambridge University Footlights Dramatic Club.

Jonny Sweet grew up in Nottingham and was educated at Nottingham High School, a fee-paying establishment that caters for children as young as 4 up to 18. Famous people who have graced Nottingham High School include politicians Ed Balls and Kenneth Clarke and renowned writer D.H. Lawrence.

Career

Once through High School, Sweet read English at Pembroke College, Cambridge. It was at Cambridge where Jonny would cut his teeth in the comedy world by meeting up with Simon Bird and Joe Thomas and follow in the footsteps of other Pembroke alumni, such as Peter Cook and Eric Idle.

As Vice President of the Footlights performing-arts club, he, Bird and Thomas would start to forge their path through the comedy world with their show the *House of Windsor* and at the Edinburgh Fringe Festival they would gain critical acclaim for their three-man show *The Meeting*. After tasting success in Edinburgh, Sweet was to then fly solo before reconnecting with the lads. In 2009 Jonny won the Edinburgh Comedy Award for Best Newcomer for his one-man show 'Mostly About Arthur', in which Sweet waxes lyrical about his deceased brother. We've dug out an old review by Sophie Vukovic from *festmag.co.uk*, who describes the show that won him the prestigious award, whose former winners include Harry Hill, Tim Vine and *The Mighty Boosh*.

'You're definitely my favourite five people in here!' gushes Jonny Sweet to groups of his audience entering his show *Mostly About Arthur*. Affable and unabashedly middle-class, with a Cambridge Footlights background, Sweet's somewhat toff-like demeanour is instantly engaging. The show is a bizarre elegy to his deceased brother, blurb author extraordinaire Arthur (assumed fictional), and it creates a wonderfully inventive world, coloured with wickedly silly tales.

Sweet giggles and flusters his way through a slideshow illustrating his brother's life like a schoolboy at show and tell, before getting to the show's unequivocal highlight: the transformation of the stage into a Starbucks, for a biopic of Arthur. Sweet employs members of the audience as actors/props, while he plays the pretentious director, further playing up to his public school persona as he quips, 'You obviously haven't trained at RADA!'

Sweet made a name for himself doing sketches as part of comedy trio House of Windsor, and his penchant for sketch comedy is evident. Creating these surreal scenarios arguably takes more creativity than gags based on schadenfreude, stereotypes or the use of innuendo to elicit embarrassed chortles.

After a brief cameo in *The Inbetweeners* ('Night out in London' episode), Jonny Sweet would continue his posh-boy style by playing David Cameron in the Channel 4 one-off *When Boris*

Met Dave, a comedy about Boris Johnson and David Cameron in their Eton and Oxford University days. The show was narrated by Antony Head (of *Buffy the Vampire Slayer* fame and, of course, father of our very own Carli D'Amato, played by Emily Head). Alongside Sweet's portrayal of David Cameron, Christian Brassington played Boris Johnson.

In 2010 Jonny would continue on his lonesome by performing in *Pete & Dud: The Lost Sketches*, a BBC2 comedy where contemporary comedians would recreate a series of sketches written by Peter Cook and Dudley Moore between 1965 and 1970. Other notable comedians in the show included Jonathan Ross, Simon Day, Hugh Dennis, Adrian Edmondson, Alistair McGowan, Stephen Fry and David Mitchell. The show received mixed reviews from the critics who, on the whole, enjoyed the quality of the gags but felt they lacked the delivery of the original writers.

Onwards and upwards, Jonny continued to make his way on his own and, after recording a pilot for *Chickens* in 2011, he appeared in an episode of the acclaimed BBC comedy *Twenty Twelve*, a satire about the London 2012 Olympic Games, which starred Hugh Bonneville, Amelia Bullmore and Jessica Hynes.

After finally being reunited with Simon Bird and Joe Thomas, Jonny played the character of Ian in the final series of *Him & Her* while the first series of *Chickens* was airing on Sky 1.

In 2014 he played the character of Superintendent Tom Oliver in the comedy drama *Babylon* on Channel 4. Directed by Danny Boyle, *Babylon* took a humorous look at the modern-day police force using original and unorthodox filming methods. The show starred Brit Marling, an American writer and actress, and James Nesbitt, renowned Northern Irish actor whose credits include *Bloody Sunday*, *Cold Feet*, *Murphy's Law,* and *Monroe*, to name a few.

So it seems Jonny Sweet likes to dip in and out of his Footlights past and who can blame him? Expect to see more 'toffcomedy' in the future, whether it's utilising the services of Simon Bird and Joe Thomas, or flying solo in mini-projects of his own. All we know is, with a name like Jonny Sweet, the world is your oyster!

Damon Beesley & Iain Morris

Thank you Damon and Iain! They gave the world *The Inbetweeners*, so it's only fair that we dedicate a section of the book especially to them! Rumours were rife about whether they would make another film and, luckily for us, they decided to take the plunge. Naturally, fans of the show were excited when they announced that the official release of the new film would be 6 August 2014. In an interview with *Digital Spy*, Damon and Iain said they were also thrilled about the project:

> We couldn't be more excited to be making another *Inbetweeners* movie with Simon, Joe, James and Blake. Frankly it's pathetic how much we've all missed each other. A new chapter in the lives of the Inbetweeners feels like the very least we can do to thank the fans for their phenomenal response to the first movie.

Background & Careers

Both Damon and Iain started their careers writing and producing for various TV and radio shows in the UK from the late 1990s. Iain worked on XFM, co-hosting a show with comedian Jimmy Carr before both Damon and Iain hooked up on the satirical Channel 4 production *The 11 O'Clock Show* and consequently moved into a flat together. After dabbling with various other productions together, they pitched the idea of *The Inbetweeners* to bosses at Channel 4, who commissioned the programme for a six-part series to air in 2008. After the show began on the Channel 4 sister-channel E4, both writers revealed that many of the awkward moments and gags in the show had actually come from their own experiences growing up, and this technique of writing what you know about has proved to be a success, not just to Beesley and Morris but also to their good friends Ricky Gervais and Stephen Merchant. Interestingly, during the writing process, Iain Morris revealed to Radio 5 that he spent a part of a year writing the show while living in David Walliams's flat rent free. 'That allowed me to write. Without David Walliams, and another friend who also let me stay for free for nine months, I probably wouldn't have been able to continue to try and write stuff.'

Three series of the show were made and the critics raved about it and thus the awards came streaming in between 2008 and 2010, including Best New TV Comedy at the 2008 British Comedy Awards and Best Situation Comedy at the 2009 British Academy Television Awards. In the summer of 2011 the first film was made and ended up being one of the biggest-grossing British comedies of all time, bringing in £41 million at the box office. *Empire* magazine asked the writers about the film and what it was like to write a British comedy film: 'The series has been successful around the world by us making it British and about a particularly British set of youths and people seem to get it.' Damon added that people in this country seem to gravitate towards British culture:

> I think it works on two levels, I think people like 'peeking over the wall' and watching and listening to what boys that age are really like and what they say about the world, and there should be a fascination with Brits abroad, I know that we're genuinely fascinated with ourselves abroad and I do think that the rest of the world might find that interesting too.

After writing and producing the first film, Beesley and Morris announced that they would not only be writing the sequel but that this time they would also be directing it, a role that was given to Ben Palmer in the first film.

Not that it matters so much considering the film did so well at the box office but let's take a look at what the critics thought of the film:

'Gags about sex, vomit and hand shandies are all present and correct as our anti-heroes struggle with the challenges of being abroad and meeting girls. Think the English version of *American Pie*.' Carol Carter and Larushka Ivan-Zadeh, *Metro*.

'Beneath the gross language, the poo jokes, and the childish behaviour, it is an extremely accurate and almost emotional study of the relationship between teenage boys, the way they find it hard to express affection except through abuse, their abiding loyalty to their mates, their essential difficulties in growing up.' Sarah Crompton, *The Daily Telegraph*.

'They drink, they say "cock" a lot, they wear bright-pink T-shirts with "Pussay Patrol" emblazoned on them, they fumble about with a quartet of English girls and they are threatened by a Greek waiter and a handsome studmuffin. All the traits and trappings of a typically decadent British holiday, then.' Derek Adams, *Time Out*.

Along with *The Inbetweeners*, Damon and Iain have also worked on a number of other comedy shows, including *Flight of the Conchords*, *Look Around You* and the Radio 4 comedy show *So Wrong it's Right*, alongside comedian Charlie Brooker. In their personal lives, both Damon and Iain are married, with Iain having married American singer and DJ Marchelle Bradanini on 14 May 2011. His best man on the day was, of course, none other than his writing partner Damon Beesley.

Twitter

It's not only the actors who are getting involved in the Twitter scene. Iain Morris has over 25,000 followers and has tweeted over 16,000 times, mostly responding to fans and retweeting fellow comedians, such as Ricky Gervais. What has he been babbling on about under the guise of @iainkevanmorris? Let's take a look:

'it's always been my dream to watch a boxing day test at the MCG and this year i get to go. hooray. lucky me. great.' Iain plans some recreational activities while filming the new *Inbetweeners* movie.

'please watch Drifters by @jessicaknappett this evening on E4. i promise you'll laugh and she did it all herself.' Iain bigs up the comedy show he helped to produce.

'Suarez 10 games for a bite trying to get someone off him, what should Torres get for unprovoked gouge to face? 20?' A rare bit of football banter from Iain.

'Murray's double-fisted backhand is turning something designed for ladies into something frighteningly masculine. just like a kilt.' Iain makes a striking analogy while watching Andy Murray in the final of Wimbledon 2013.

'to confirm – YOGA. You'll feel a bit of a dick during, but after it's all good. (i think that's the slogan).' Iain gets fully into life living in Los Angeles.

Unfortunately, we couldn't find any sign of Damon Beesley on Twitter. Maybe we should start a campaign to get him involved, as Iain seems to be taking all of the limelight!

Ben Palmer
Background
Ben Palmer is a British director, writer and producer. He is famous for working on a number of British TV and comedy shows and has directed 11 episodes of *The Inbetweeners*, as well as *The Inbetweeners Movie*, and an episode of *Chickens*.

Career
Let's take a look in more detail at Ben Palmer's work.

Bo Selecta (2002–04) – Ben directed 23 episodes of the comedy-sketch show created by Leigh Francis. The show featured Francis playing a number of characters, wearing a latex mask that loosely resembled them! The most popular characters on the show were Mel B, Craig David, Elton John and Michael Jackson.

A Bear's Tail (2005) – One of the spin-off shows from *Bo Selecta* was the character of a small bear who interviewed star guests and was inexplicably rude to them before exposing himself! The show featured Patsy Kensit, Kelly Osborne and

Davina McCall, either playing themselves or exaggerated versions of themselves.

Keith Lemon's Very Brilliant World Tour (2008) – Ben continued working with Leigh Francis to develop one of his other characters, Keith Lemon. In this show, Keith would travel around the world interviewing special guest stars, such as Mel C and Mel B, Holly Valance, Holly Willoughby, Sharon Osborne and Dermot O'Leary.

Star Stories (2008) – Ben directed five episodes of the impression show, which aired for three series from 2006–08. Each episode focused on a particular celebrity story but featured a number of other characters too, which were played by comedy performers that included Kevin Bishop, Steve Edge and Harry Peacock. Ben directed the episodes 'Elton John', 'Heather Mills', 'Peter Andre & Jordan', 'Kate Moss' and 'Bono'.

Comedy Lab (2004–2010) – *Comedy Lab* was a British TV series that showcased experimental shows with a view to them spawning series in their own right. Shows which were born into *Comedy Lab* include *Trigger Happy TV*, *Fonejacker* and *That Peter Kay Thing*. In 2004 Ben was VT director for *The Russell Brand* and in 2010 he directed the episodes 'Penelope Princess of Pets' and 'Filth'.

The Inbetweeners (2009–10) – All in all, Ben directed 11 episodes of the show: 'The Field Trip', 'Work Experience', 'Will's Birthday', 'Night Out in London', 'The Duke of Edinburgh Awards', 'Exam Time', 'The Fashion Show', 'The Gig and the Girlfriend', 'Will's Dilemma', 'Trip to Warwick' and 'Will is Home Alone'.

The Inbetweeners Movie (2011) – As *The Inbetweeners* series became a smash hit on TV, Ben was chosen to direct the movie.

While on the red carpet, Ben told reporters about his thoughts on the show and life on set:

> I think we're really lucky, the show has really hit home and has such a fan base. They helped us out a lot in creating scenes that we shouldn't have been able to achieve with the budget we had. The boys were brilliant [Simon, Joe, James, Blake]. It's hard to be a sensible director around them!

As plans were being drawn together for the sequel to the film, Ben was not in the running, as writers Iain Morris and Damon Beesley would be directing it themselves.

Comedy Showcase (2012) – From 2007–12 Channel 4 produced one-off comedy shows featuring some of Britain's fledgling talent. Those shows that have gone on to be commissioned for a full series include *The Kevin Bishop Show*, *PhoneShop*, *The Increasingly Poor Decisions of Todd Margaret* and *Chickens*. Ben directed the episode *House of Rooms*, a sitcom about a mother and son duo who rent rooms in their large house to various tenants. Ben also directed the pilot episode *Milton Jones' House of Rooms*, which was never commissioned for a full series.

Them from That Thing (2012) – This TV mini-series was shown over two parts on Channel 4 and featured a raft of comedy stars in a sketch-show format. One of the show's regular stars was Blake Harrison and he, along with Kayvan Novak, Sally Phillips and Morgana Robinson, would be joined by other comedians and TV personalities. Ben directed both episodes, which were shown on consecutive nights in August 2012.

Bad Sugar (2012) – Ben directed this comedy pilot, which was a spoof melodrama series aimed at making fun of over-the-top soap operas – those that are particularly popular in Latin America. The show had some big comedy names, including Olivia Colman, Julia Davies and Peter Serafinowicz, to name a few, and was commissioned for a full series after the pilot, only for it to then be cancelled. The reason for the cancellation was apparently due to difficulties over coordinating the schedules of the main actors involved.

Chickens (2013) – Ben teamed up with fellow *Inbetweeners* actors Simon Bird and Joe Thomas, along with Jonny Sweet, on their project *Chickens*. In an interview with *British Comedy Guide*, he spoke about the challenges when working on the set of the comedy show:

> The fact it's a period piece comes with a mountain of challenges. When you're doing something set in 1914, everything becomes that little bit harder. I was really keen for the village to be as large a character as the three boys, so finding a village that felt authentic was a tough act to pull off, not to mention making the production design and costumes true to that time. Against that, though, the boys' writing has got a modern vernacular, a pacey, contemporary style, and my instinct was to shoot it with a handheld, fluid camera to give it a quirky look, not to play to period conventions. We made life very difficult for ourselves [laughs].

London Irish (2013) – Another Channel 4 project that Ben worked on was this comedy series about four Northern Irish friends living and working in London. Ben directed the second episode in the first series, which was written by Lisa McGee, an

Irish stage-and-screen writer whose credits include *Totally Frank* and *Being Human*.

Man Up (2014) – The very latest project for Ben is directing the British rom-com *Man Up*, starring Simon Pegg and Lake Bell, which started shooting in January 2014 and is due for release in the same year. Simon Pegg, of course, is famous for films such as *Shaun of the Dead*, *Hot Fuzz* and *The Adventures of Tintin*. However, Lake Bell is a little less known in the UK. She has appeared in many American TV shows, including *New Girl* and *Boston Legal*. She was also a voice in the 2014 animated film *Mr Peabody & Sherman*.

In an interview with *British Comedy Guide*, Ben told of his pet hates when it comes to directing:

> Running out of time [laughs]. You never, ever have enough time. The other thing is being underprepared. I once made the mistake of being unprepared, not knowing where I should put the camera next and, now, I'm a stickler for huge amounts of prep and knowing exactly what I need to do. Even if you change it on the day, at least you've got the plan to fall back on.

The future certainly looks bright for Ben and he's done a great job in making *The Inbetweeners* look fantastic, so hopefully he'll be teaming up with the lads again in the future.

CHAPTER FOUR

LIFE AFTER THE INBETWEENERS

The Inbetweeners has been a fruitful project for many of the actors in the series, not just for the four main characters; it has also propelled the careers of some of the bit-part actors who had small roles but were pivotal in the plot circulating around Will, Simon, Jay and Neil. Outlined here are some of the key projects that provided life after *The Inbetweeners*.

Fresh Meat

When the creators of *Peep Show*, Sam Bain and Jesse Armstrong, came up with the new comedy *Fresh Meat*, the role of awkward fresher Kingsley Owen was suited perfectly to *Inbetweeners* star Joe Thomas.

The writers were inspired by 1980s cult classic *The Young Ones*, creating the characters and writing the first episode while watching the series, and this can clearly be seen in the show, which follows a group of six students at the fictional Manchester Medlock University who, after applying late to stay in the university halls of residence, are forced into a house-share on the edge of the city.

In the award-winning show, Thomas's character is a geology student and, much like his *Inbetweeners* character, Kingsley is unlucky in love and an awkward, inexperienced young man who often finds himself in situations beyond his control.

One of the main plots across the show's several series is Kingsley's romance (or lack of romance) with fellow housemate Josie. The pair clearly like each other right from the off but, for one reason or another, things don't work out until the third series (after his fling with drama student Ruth), when the two finally hook up. But even then, things aren't quite perfect.

In an interview with *Radio Times*, Thomas explained that, despite the couple (described as the new Ross and Rachel) looking like they're meant to be together, he thinks the audience don't really want things to go smoothly:

I think people do want them to get together but dramatically it relies on it not going right. There is nothing more boring than a happy couple. People don't want that, really. If you look on Facebook and someone's said, 'I just love my husband SO much,' I'm always like, 'When is death? When do I get to kill myself?' It's just boring, but I do think they are good together and I think he wants her.

The cast working alongside the *Inbetweeners* star are also top notch; a mix of new and familiar faces.

Candice

Fresher Candice is a home-schooled ingénue who's never heard of sun-dried tomatoes or Simon Cowell. She becomes the latest housemate at 28 Hartnell Avenue, where Oregon claims her as her protégé.

Not one of the original 'Fresh Meaters', Candice joins the show in the third series. She's very impressionable and looks up to the more experienced students in the house, taking up feminism, Christianity and becoming a goth, in her quest to find individuality and to fit in. Makes sense!

Howard

Our favourite character, Howard, played by Scottish actor and writer Greg McHugh, isn't like the others. As the only non-fresher in the house, you'd expect Howard to be able to point out all of the best places to go, the best things to do and the most popular people to know to the other housemates but this isn't the case at all.

After dropping out of his first course, Philosophy, following a disagreement with a lecturer and then taking up Geology, Howard is a bit of a loner. In the first series of the show he's almost an enigma, skirting in and out of our screens with his socially inept qualities but, as the show develops and he forms friendships with the others, he becomes a little more relaxed, albeit just as whacky!

J.P.

The extremely posh Jonathan Pembersley (or 'JP', as he insists on being known) is well out of his comfort zone in the house after failing to get into a more respected university.

At the start of the first series the ex-public schoolboy, played by up-and-coming comedian Jack Whitehall, considers himself a god among men in the house and his snooty personality doesn't go down too well with the others. But once he realises they're not impressed by his James Cartwright-esque bullshit, JP calms things down, even buying the student house after the death of his father, so that the gang can all stick together through uni.

Josie

Juliet to Kingsley's Romeo, Josie is played by Welsh actress Kimberley Nixon. University life starts well for Josie, despite her failing relationship with her boyfriend then fiancé Dave back home; she's enjoying the big nights out after leaving a small town in Wales and her dentistry course is just what she wants to do.

But all this changes when, after a big night out, Josie turns up to a practical exam hungover and ends up drilling through a patient's cheek. Ouch! Obviously, Josie gets kicked off the course for this and, with Kingsley dating one of her friends, Heather, and her having to move to Southampton University, it looks like things are never going to kick off for the pair.

She has something of a complicated relationship with Kingsley. Although they're attracted to each other, he's dating one of her friends. Plus, there's the fact that she has to relocate to Southampton to continue her studies... this time in Zoology!?!

This goes on until the third series, when the pair finally start to get their act together. Both single(ish), they give the whole relationship thing a go but when it finally happens, it doesn't really happen and, after several attempts to fix their issues, the couple decide that being just friends is the best option. We're sure there's more to come from the two though.

Oregon

Melissa 'Oregon' Shawcross, like JP, comes from a much more privileged background than the other housemates. A fresher looking for a fresh start, the literature student uses university as her chance to reinvent herself, taking on the nickname Oregon and hanging round with drug-taking, party-animal housemate Vod.

In her attempt to really break away from the establishment, Oregon ends up getting involved with her married lecturer Tony Shales, much to the annoyance of Vod. Things don't work out for the couple and, without realising, she later ends up in a relationship with his son Dylan!

Vod

Last but by no means least there's Violet 'Vod' Nordstrom, played by actress and playwright Zawe Ashton. Vod takes student life to the extreme. Her days consist more of binge drinking and drug taking than getting involved in her studies.

Her coolness and anti-establishment views impress the other housemates at the same time as almost scaring them and it's very rare that we see any real emotion from her. In the third series, Vod ends up in a holiday romance that somehow almost ends up with a wedding! She eventually realises she needs to sort this out, as she certainly isn't ready to settle down, and sends the guy packing. It's after this incident that we realise just why Vod is so troubled, when the gang meet her alcoholic mother. The guys are initially impressed by her mum Chris's partying attitude but they soon realise it's a problem and later find out that, as a kid, Vod was really badly treated, so they rally round their housemate to comfort her.

Reviews

'As you'd expect from the creators of *Peep Show*, this university comedy is a cut above – and the third series was the slickest to date. Jack Whitehall was born to play JP, the show's fabulously self-centred posho (he'd prefer "ledge").' The *Radio Times*.

'Just when you're wondering if *Fresh Meat* is losing its way, you'll notice the relentlessly amusing dialogue, the superb characterisation and the fine performances.' Phil Harrison, *Time Out*.

'*Fresh Meat* has attracted a reliable audience with its lazy student shibboleths – the obsession with sex and partying, the disdain for housework – but if you took out the coarseness, erections and cynicism you could almost be watching *Friends*, a show about hugging.' Phil Hogan, the *Observer*.

It's no surprise that, with such a great cast and storylines viewers can really relate to, *Fresh Meat* has become a massive hit. Opening to a great reception, things went from strength to strength for the show, which won Best New Comedy in 2011 at the British Comedy Awards, Best TV Show at the 2012 NME Awards, Best Scripted Comedy and Best Writer – Comedy at the Royal Television Society Awards, among others! We just hope there's another series on its way soon.

Friday Night Dinner

Friday Night Dinner is a British sitcom centring on the lives of a Jewish family (and their unusual neighbours) who regularly meet around the dinner table. The series was created and written by Robert Popper, who draws on his own experiences of growing up in a Jewish family. *Friday Night Dinner* stars Inbetweener Simon Bird, who plays Adam Goodman, a 20-something budding musician and the elder of two sons in the family. Simon recalls to *mirror.co.uk* one scene where onscreen brother Jonny has to pretend to bite him: 'We were filming a scene where Tom has to lunge for me as if to bite me and in the episode it cuts away, but in reality he did actually bite me and nearly drew blood. I never got him back but fingers crossed for another series and I shall get him back.' The sitcom also stars Tamsin Greig, Paul Ritter, Tom Rosenthal and Mark Heap.

As with many British sitcoms, *Friday Night Dinner* was given an American makeover in 2011 when Greg Daniels (American comedy writer and producer) picked up the series for a pilot. However, the remake was not commissioned for a full series in the USA.

After two successful series in Britain, in 2011 and 2012, a third series was aired in 2014.

What They Said
Simon Bird was asked by *TV Choice* magazine if anyone had said *Friday Night Dinner* reminded them of their own family:

Yeah, definitely. I think that's why we did the show in the first place, and why Robert Popper [*Friday Night Dinner*'s writer and producer] wanted to write it. This is Channel 4's way of doing a family sitcom. It's based on Robert's real family, and I think that comes across. You can tell when sitcoms are written based on real experience, and this one definitely is. That's really important – a big part of its success.

Bird also told *collider.com* that his character Adam is similar but slightly different to that of Will McKenzie. 'I think Adam is more comfortable in his own skin, so there's no direct overlap. Any overlap is just my own idea to make the character distinct. I think Adam is certainly more comfortable and put together, and less vulgar.'

Reviews

'*Friday Night Dinner* features a fictional Jewish family from North London, and I'm still not sure whether the programme is comedy or tragedy. Either way though, it's increasingly watchable.' Victor Lewis-Smith, the *Independent*.

'Hello bambinos! The most underrated show on TV and also quite probably the funniest. Great performances all round, but (topless) Paul Ritter and Mark Heap steal the show every week.' Alex Fletcher, *Digital Spy*.

'Part of the reason why *Friday Night Dinner* seems to work is the fact that it's based on something real, namely the actual experiences of such "Friday night dinners" of the writer Robert Popper. It gives the show an extra footing from which you can get more laughs, and it does seems to work.' Ian Wolf, *Giggle Beats*.

The Look of Love

The 2013 film *The Look of Love* stars Steve Coogan and was directed by Michael Winterbottom. The film is a biopic of Paul Raymond, a British businessman who made money through nightclubs and property. The film circulates around the life of Raymond, who enters into a Playboy lifestyle and nurtures his daughter with a view to her taking over the business. The film also featured Anna Friel as Paul Raymond's wife and Imogen Poots as his daughter.

Simon Bird has a small part in the film, playing the character of Jonathan Hodge. Other notable cast members include David Walliams, Matt Lucas, Stephen Fry and Miles Jupp.

Reviews

'*The Look of Love* is a disappointingly crude and shallow biography of the self-made northern impresario Paul Raymond, who started out conducting a music hall mind-reading act and finished up as a multi-millionaire nightclub proprietor, pornographer, owner of much of Soho, and for a while the richest man in Britain.' Phillip French, *The Guardian*.

'A solid, straightforward biopic about a fascinating individual and his destructive relationships, with strong performances and a healthy sense of naffness.' Dan Jolin, *Empire Online*.

'[Michael]Winterbottom and cinematographer Hubert Taczanowski lovingly evoke the look and feel of London through the decades. Still there's something a bit over-familiar here – in a solidly entertaining, made-for-telly, nothing-we-haven't-seen-before, way. And given that the last time Coogan and Winterbottom worked together it was on the genius-funny road-trip comedy series *The Trip*, you can't help wishing for something a little sharper.' Cath Clarke, *Time Out*.

Chickens

Chickens is written by and features *Inbetweeners* stars Simon Bird and Joe Thomas, along with their Cambridge University writing colleague Jonny Sweet. The sitcom is set during World War I and is directed by *The Inbetweeners Movie* director Ben Palmer. The series revolves around three males – Cecil, George and Bert – who have dodged the war effort by either feigning injuries or pure laziness and find themselves as the only men in a small village.

The show was originally aired in 2011 as part of Channel 4's *Comedy Showcase* and in 2013 Sky1 commissioned a six-episode first series.

As *Chickens* is probably the most important piece of comedy for our *Inbetweeners* alumni, we thought we would give a short synopsis of each of the episodes, without giving too much away, of course!

Episode 1

It's wartime in Rittle-On-Sea and George, Bert and Cecil are looking for ways to keep peace with the women in the local community, who have already disregarded them as outcasts for dodging the war. Cecil joins a local knitting club, George, in an effort to keep his future wife happy, agrees to write arousing letters to soldiers on the front line and Bert's pursuit of any woman with a pulse in the village begins with him having sex with Cecil's sister after she decides she must have regular intercourse while her husband is away.

Episode 2

There's more hate mail from the Rittle residents but that's the least of the fellas' problems, as the house they share is now producing brown water from the tap – not ideal when all of the tradesmen in the town are off fighting for their country! In an effort to do their bit for the community, Bert and Cecil pay their respects to a dead soldier at a memorial service. However, things take an odd turn when Bert decides to chase the grieving widow. Meanwhile, as the last male teacher in the village and a pacifist, George finds it difficult to punish a disobedient child.

Episode 3
Bert winds up the lads one time too many and finds himself out on his ear after an incident involving a lack of toilet paper and a romantic note written from George to his fiancée Winky. Meanwhile, Cecil finds himself a love interest but George and Bert are suspicious that she may have ulterior motives.

Episode 4
When the gents find themselves at the local pub doing the quiz, Cecil discovers that the women of the village are treating him a little differently, almost as one of their own. Bert finds a job working at George's school as a teacher and employs some rather unorthodox teaching methods.

Episode 5
George decides that he should invite the local village leper over for dinner, much to the joy of Bert, who decides to have a bath ready for their guest! Unfortunately, Miss Trimble stands them up and Cecil decides that, despite her highly contagious skin condition, he will win her friendship.

Episode 6
The soldiers are back in Rittle-On-Sea and Cecil, Bert and

George are over the moon to finally have some male company to bond with other than themselves. However, the male-bonding session doesn't really work out to plan; Cecil struggles to reconnect with the lads from before they went to war, George tries to convince a soldier to become an objector and Bert gets his comeuppance when his antics come back to haunt him.

What They Said
Joe Thomas and Jonny Sweet described the show in an interview with the *British Comedy Guide*.

Joe: 'The show is set in World War One and it's about the men who stayed behind and didn't fight. Cecil, George and Bert are the only three men left in the village and all the women hate them. That's pretty much the gist of it.'

Jonny: 'Each of us has a different reason for not going to war: Bert doesn't know what's going on; Cecil wants to go to war, but has flat feet and is very disappointed he can't go; and George is a pacifist, so he's against the war. It's just three guys staying at home while lots of other men are being brave and heroic.'

In the same interview, Joe Thomas, Simon Bird and Jonny Sweet all describe their characters and the troubles they have in the series.

Joe: 'My character, George, the main source of pain in his life is that his relationship is falling apart because he hasn't joined the army. He's torn between his principles and what social etiquette dictates, and his fiancée's friends have stopped respecting her because of her choice of husband. George isn't a combative man and he doesn't want to rub people up the wrong way, but he has and now he doesn't know what to do about it.'

Simon: 'Cecil, in a nutshell, is undergoing an existential crisis.

He is desperate to go to war, but isn't allowed to and, because of that he's paralysed with fear about what people think about him. His story is one of constantly trying to convince the rest of the village that he genuinely did want to sign up. It's a losing battle, though, because he is automatically associated with these two, one of whom is vehemently anti-war, and the other one doesn't really know the war is going on.'

Jonny: 'Bert has got obstacles and problems on a much smaller scale – it's like a dog trying to get into a packet of biscuits while there is a fire going on around him. These two have fundamental, genuine problems with their lives and one of those is Bert.'

Reviews

'*Chickens* may be vulnerable to the suggestion that it's merely *The Inbetweeners* transferred to the First World War, but that scarcely matters as it continues to deliver the laughs. The set-up of humiliated young men and the gulf between themselves and the unimpressed opposite sex works just fine here.' David Stubs, *The Guardian*.

'It's so slight it's in danger of drifting away on the lightest breeze. But in a year when the best TV has generally ranged between solemn and devastating, it feels good to have something as blithe, breezy and just plain daft as *Chickens* to provide some light relief.' Paul Harrison, *Time Out*.

'I was really looking forward to *Chickens*, Sky1's take on British conscientious objectors during the Great War. It sounded a bold, brave and original concept that promised to push the world of *Blackadder Goes Forth* to a further level of dark, dangerous, edgy and disturbing satire. How could it fail to do otherwise, with protagonists who would have permanently existed in the shadow of public contempt, scorn and opprobrium?' Harry Venning, *The Stage*.

The Harry Hill Movie

One of Britain's favourite comedians and personalities took his crazy antics to the big screen in 2013 with *The Harry Hill Movie*. The plot of the film sees Harry Hill travel on a road trip to Blackpool with his grandmother (played by Julie Walters) when he discovers that his hamster only has a week to live. Other stars in *The Harry Hill Movie* include Matt Lucas, who plays Harry's long lost brother; Simon Bird, who plays the vet who diagnoses the hamster's critical illness; Sheridan Smith (*Two Pints of Lager and a Packet of Crisps* and *Gavin & Stacey* fame) as Michelle, Harry's love interest; Johnny Vegas, who plays Abu, Harry's hamster; and Jim Broadbent, who plays a cleaner at a nuclear power station.

The film itself was written by Harry Hill and directed by Steve Bendelack. Although you would be hard pushed to find anyone who dislikes Harry Hill, the film was not well received by the critics!

Reviews

'It's surreal, for sure, but the kind of surrealism that makes you sink lower and lower in your seat, wondering whether to make a dash for the exit.

'If you do sit it out, though, there's some enjoyment to be had in spotting the comedy references – to *The Goodies*, *The Lavender Hill Mob*, even Charlie Chaplin's *City Lights*. But I'm afraid that serves mainly to remind us what good comedy is, and what this isn't.' Brian Viner, the *Daily Mail*.

'Harry Hill's big screen debut is a bit of a misfire. Hill's humour has always had a random and surreal quality but the screenplay here isn't so much offbeat as utterly feeble.' Geoffrey MacNab, *The Independent*.

'There's not enough here to sustain 88 minutes, too many of the jokes fall flat and the image of Julie Walters rapping isn't one you'll be able to shift soon. There will be those who find *The Harry Hill Movie* about as amusing as a trip to the dentist. They're wrong.' Tom Huddleston, *Time Out*.

Rock & Chips

Rock & Chips is the prequel to the hugely successful British sitcom *Only Fools and Horses*. It features James Buckley, who plays a young Derek 'Del-Boy' Trotter set in 1960s Peckham. The three-part spin-off was originally aired in 2010 and was written by *Only Fools and Horses* writer John Sullivan and featured Nicholas Lyndhurst, who most famously starred as Rodney, as the character of Freddie Robdal.

After the show was aired, the critics did not take kindly to the spin-off but many were favourable to James Buckley's role at Del-Boy. Keith Watson, in *Metro*, suggested this of Buckley and Kellie Bright (who played Joan Trotter, Del-Boy's mother): 'They deserved a show all to themselves.' One of many favourable reviews for the pair.

What They Said

Nicholas Lyndhurst told *bbc.co.uk* about his time working with James Buckley:

The team were very clever in casting all the young characters as they cast them not as individuals, but together, to see how they pinged off each other and what kind of chemistry they had. And, of course, they're all brilliant together. Not one of them tried to caricature what anyone did previously in *Fools* and they all bring a completely fresh appeal.

Buckley himself has made no secret of his love for *Only Fools and Horses* and, in preparation for the part, he purchased the complete box set of the show. He said this about the prospect of playing a young Del-Boy: 'There was no pressure to imitate David Jason and I don't think anyone would have wanted that. It's just important to remember that this isn't an episode of *Only Fools And Horses*. That's already been done and so brilliantly that there wouldn't be any point in trying to do it again. This is completely different and I think, as long as people realise this is something new and exciting, they'll get a lot out of it.'

Reviews

'[the storyline] virtually abandoned its main character [the young Del-Boy] and its best actor [the engaging James Buckley from *The Inbetweeners*] who played him.' Jim Shelly, the *Daily Mirror*.

'The thing you have to remember when watching *Rock & Chips* is not to treat it as a sitcom but as a comedy drama. There are no real belly laughs, but a few chuckles along the way. At times it is rather tender. It is also ruder. I cannot recall an episode of *Only Fools* which included the phrase: "F★★★ off".' Ian Wolf, *Giggle Beats*.

'It may not be remembered as the late great John Sullivan's finest work, but *Rock & Chips* still wipes the floor with most of the dross drama we have to put up with. Packed with great one-liners, BBC1's *Only Fools and Horses* prequel is what feel-good telly is all about.' Kevin O'Sullivan, the *Mirror*.

Him & Her

Him & Her was a hugely successful BBC3 sitcom that featured the lives of two main characters, Steve and Becky (played by Russell Tovey and Sarah Solemani). The premise of the story revolved around all of the scenes being shot in their one-bedroom flat, where friends, family and neighbours would often appear. The show ran for four series, with the fourth and final series culminating in the pair getting married.

The show was written by Stefan Golaszewski, a fellow Cambridge Floodlights alumni member with Simon Bird and Joe Thomas.

Blake Harrison joins the cast for an episode in season one and in season two as Barney, Steve's friend.

What They Said

'I was by no means making a living out of this [comedy writing] and I thought it would be kind of nice to write a sitcom where it's two people and they never leave their bedroom.' Writer Stefan Golaszewski talks to *British Comedy Guide* about how the idea for *Him & Her* came about.

Reviews

'*Him & Her* is by the far the best sitcom to have ever landed up on BBC3, and surely the only one with roots in Harold Pinter.

Observational comedy is an over-used term, but this was the real McCoy.' Gerard Gilbert, *The Independent*.

'Much of this last episode takes place in the toilet – as befits one of the grossest comedies ever to grace the small screen. It's also gloriously uncouth: the mangy neighbour glugs the dregs of drinks, the bride's father rubs up against one of the bridesmaids, the sozzled bride rubs up against anyone in trousers.' Claire Webb, *Radio Times*.

'If there's a more excruciating half hour of comedy on offer this year than last night's *Him & Her: The Wedding*, then please don't make me watch it. Till death do they part might come sooner than we think.' Keith Watson, *Metro*.

The Increasingly Poor Decisions of Todd Margaret

The Increasingly Poor Decisions of Todd Margaret featured Blake Harrison in one of his first main roles since leaving *The Inbetweeners*. The story revolves around the life of Todd, who finds himself heading up the UK office of an energy-drink company. With no experience of running a company or knowledge of British culture, the show guides the viewers through his misplaced experiences and decisions. The show ran for two series in 2010 and 2012 and Blake Features in all 12 episodes. However, the outcome could have been entirely different: in the pilot episode, his character Dave was played by Russell Tovey, who would later go on to play Steve in *Him & Her*.

The Increasingly Poor Decisions of Todd Margaret was written by David Cross, an American comedy writer famous for his roles in *Arrested Development* and the ABC sitcom *Modern Family*.

What They Said

Blake Harrison spoke to *Digital Spy* before the first series aired in the UK:

> This show has some amazing people in it, I mean anyone who has seen *Arrested Development* will know how good Will Arnett and David Cross are. I think there are parts in the second series that are personally the best thing that I've ever done. It was a real challenge for me, series two, and I'm really glad people will get to see that now.

Reviews

'The first thing to say about the show is that it doesn't skimp on energy or jokes. But the energy is unfocused and the quality of the jokes fluctuates wildly throughout, depending heavily upon contrived, slapstick set pieces. Moreover, Todd's trademark haplessness frequently topples over into outright irritating, never an attractive quality in a sitcom lead character.' Harry Venning, *The Stage*.

'*The Increasingly Poor Decisions of Todd Margaret* really ought to be pressing the buttons. It's got the cast (David Cross, Sharon Horgan, Will Arnett) and the prestige but, two episodes in, it's sorely lacking gags and sympathy for its protagonist.' *The Guardian*.

'Though spottily amusing, it's a disappointment overall, especially given the track record of Cross and Will Arnett, a fellow *Arrested Development* alumnus who cameos as Todd's monstrously priapic, foul-mouthed boss.' Paul Whitelaw, *The Scotsman*.

White Van Man

White Van Man is a British sitcom written by Adrian Poynton and starring Will Mellor as the main character, Ollie. The premise of the show follows the troubles of Ollie as he takes over the family handyman business along with his assistant Darren (played by Joel Fry). The show also features Georgia Moffett, Naomi Bentley, Clive Mantle and, of course, Blake Harrison, who plays Ricky, the local thief and somewhat of an acquaintance to Ollie.

White Van Man ran for two series on BBC3 in 2011 and 2012. In 2012 an American network picked up the sitcom for a full-series remake after a successful pilot, naming it *Family Tools*, with writer Adrian Poynton working as a consultant producer. After the first series, it was announced in 2013 that it would not be receiving a second.

What They Said

Will Mellor (who plays leading character Ollie) spoke to the *British Comedy Guide* about the quality of the writing in *White Van Man*:

> It amazed me that it was Adrian's [Poynton] writing. It came off the page so easily, which is sometimes difficult when you get a new writer. It sometimes takes a long time to get that across. He writes very good conversation, great characters and it's a very naturalistic way of writing and speaking. I found it really easy to work with his script and that's why I wanted to do the show – I was really impressed. It's different, as well, because it's got that drama element – it's not necessarily a show full of gags and jokes.

Reviews

'There ought to be mileage in a comedy based around the much maligned white van man, but on early evidence this series fails to make the most of the opportunity. It's not that it's bad, it's just that's it's not very good – or clever.' Simon Horsford, *The Daily Telegraph*.

'BBC3's new show, *White Van Man* starring Will Mellor, was a ridiculous farce which could have worked – but didn't.' Keith Watson, the *Metro*.

'It probably won't make you laugh like an unblocked drain but it's on a par with Mellor's *Two Pints Of Lager*.' Jane Simon, the *Daily Mirror*.

Way To Go

Way to Go is a British sitcom about three men who set up an assisted suicide business. The show was first aired on BBC3 in January 2013 and was originally commissioned for six thirty-minute episodes. After a first series with mixed reviews from the critics, the sitcom was decommissioned.

Blake Harrison played the main character of Scott, a receptionist at a veterinary clinic, who has dropped out of medical school, becomes short of cash and decides to set up the business with his half-brother and his friend, Joey and Cozzo, played by Ben Heathcote and Marc Wootton.

The show came with excellent credentials, as it was created by Bob Kushell, an American writer and producer whose writing credits include *The Simpsons, 3rd Rock from the Sun, Malcolm in the Middle* and *American Dad*.

The subject matter of the sitcom, assisted suicide, meant the show gathered criticism from certain people outside of comedy circles, including some British politicians, who claimed the show made light of a serious issue facing many people in the UK and across the world. Blake Harrison had this to say about the criticism when asked in an interview with *metro.co.uk*:

> If someone says something like that in regards to our show, all I can think is they haven't seen it. We deal with the subject in a sensitive way. The comedy doesn't come from suicide, it comes from the characters and the things they're involved with. I enjoyed doing the show because I got to perform a lot of the scenes, including all the suicide scenes, in a dramatic way.

What They Said

Tory MP Mark Pritchard told the *Sunday Express* about the nature of the sitcom and his distaste for the subject matter: 'It is a sad fact that assisted dying is now regarded as a "revenue stream" to some foreign clinics and clearly as a matter of fun by some parts of the BBC.'

In response to fierce criticism, Blake Harrison hit back at many people who expressed disapproval: 'The people who have a problem with it don't seem to have seen the show, which I find strange. If you're going to condemn something, you should have seen it first, otherwise it seems a bit ignorant. The writer had a debate on the radio with someone from the *Christian Voice* who hadn't seen it.'

Reviews

'This comedy about three friends trying to set up an assisted suicide business has its moments thanks to its talented cast. When it works, the mix of the dark, the absurd and the comic is very funny but crassness (maybe hard to avoid given the subject matter) sometimes gets in the way.' Simon Horsford, *The Daily Telegraph*.

'*Way to Go* isn't very "adult", the word here essentially used as a code for "involves swearing and sex". It is quite intriguing, though – a black comedy in which three friends, all down on their luck, find a new career offering euthanasia without the airfare (not so much Dignitas as Indignitas).' Tom Sutcliffe, *The Independent*.

'Watching this BBC3 sitcom is the televisual equivalent of listening to a toddler squealing "poo-poo" every five seconds because they think it's the most offensive word ever invented. *Way to Go* simply tries too hard to shock. The premise itself is controversial (and has already sparked the inevitable outrage from a Tory MP), but has plenty of potential for black humour.' Rebecca Taylor, *Time Out*.

Big Bad World

Big Bad World sees Blake Harrison play Ben Turnbull, a student who finishes university and returns to his parents' house in Great Yarmouth. As with many aspiring young graduates, Ben has to find his way in the world but first, he finds himself hanging around with his old friends, as well as trying to find a job.

The first series of *Big Bad World* aired in August 2013 on Comedy Central and was created and written by British duo Joe Tucker and Lloyd Woolf. Along with Blake Harrison, other notable stars of the show include Caroline Quentin and James Fleet, who play Ben's mother and father.

While talking to *metro.co.uk*, Blake had this to say about the series before it aired:

It'll be less controversial than *Way To Go*. It's about someone who has left university with a degree in Norse literature, can't find a job and has to move back in with his parents. His friends are in the same situation. It's topical with the number of people moving back in with their parents after university due to the recession and lack of jobs. Hopefully, people will relate to that.

What They Said

Blake spoke to *British Comedy Guide* about the atmosphere on the set of *Big Bad World* and what is was like with the other actors:

> I can say I had an absolute blast filming it. Caroline Quentin and James Fleet are just amazing – they're very funny and brilliant. As are the guys playing my friends – Seann Walsh was brilliant, particularly considering that is the first acting he has ever done! I thought he was cracking in it and he's really, really funny.

Reviews

'Despite being marred by some unnecessarily post-Partridge moments, *Big Bad World* sparks into life when it stops trying too hard and forges its own path.' Gary Rose, *Radio Times*.

'Amid the standard-issue faux pas and idle banter come a few flashes of inspiration – notably the box-ticking job interview – but surprises are generally few and the laughs gentle.' Gabriel Tate, *Time Out*.

'Right now that premise isn't translating to comedy gold, but that's not to say that it won't. The opener is rescued by a surreally tacky marriage proposal and Seann Walsh as Ben's unhygienic pal. Caroline Quentin and James Fleet milk it for all it's worth as Ben's embarrassing parents.' Mark Braxton, *Radio Times*.

Cuckoo

Cuckoo is a BBC3 comedy about the Thompson family. Ken (played by *The Inbetweeners* star Greg Davies) and Lorna (Helen Baxendale) are parents to Rachel (Tamla Kari), who comes home from a gap year married to Cuckoo, a drug-taking American hippy. The pair continue their married life by moving into the Thompson household.

The character of Cuckoo is played by Andy Samberg, an American comedian who is famous for starring in the late-night comedy-sketch show *Saturday Night Live* and is a member of the comedy group 'The Lonely Island'.

Although *Cuckoo* only ran for one series, there are rumours that a second series will run in 2014. However, it all depends on the availability of Andy Samberg, who spends most of his time in the US working on many projects.

When *comedy.co.uk* asked Greg Davies how he would react if his own daughter got married without him knowing, he said, 'I think you might be a little hurt that your child would not want you at that particular milestone but ultimately you just want those you love to be happy. I would give her my blessing and then immediately deal with my disappointment by getting drunk and giving all her inheritance away to the first stranger I met.'

In October 2013 it was announced that an American remake of *Cuckoo* would be made.

What They Said

Greg Davies talks to *British Comedy Guide* about the similarities between himself and his character Ken: 'He has my face and magnificent body. Apart from that, we're not exactly peas in a pod. He is organised and opinionated and has a plan for life. I can barely do my own shoes up. I think he is a decent chap though and – apart from that time I nicked two Yorkies from Mr Bowen's shop – I try to be.'

Andy Samberg talks to the same website about the differences between American and British humour:

Aside from the obvious cultural reference differences [Dexy's Midnight Runners?] and various common phrases, I think there's less and less difference ever year. The old line on this was that Brit humour was much wordier and dry, but this show felt very much a mix of that and some more outrageous and more 'American' comedy I've seen. Overall though, the main difference between this show and others I've done personally is that everyone in the cast and crew has an accent.'

Reviews

'The premise is exploited to the full, the scripts are consistently amusing, and the performances of Greg Davies, as the bumptious, blustering dad, and Andy Samberg, as the pseudo-spiritualist slacker son-in-law, complement each other perfectly.' Harry Venning, *The Stage*.

'I just wish *Cuckoo* was a touch funnier without relying so heavily on the performances of Samberg and Davies to raise smiles and pull it through, but I'll keep watching because it's well-made and has undeniable heart.' Dan Owen, *Dan's Media Digest*.

'But for all its contemporary setting, *Cuckoo* is a throwback to 1970s sitcoms, parents and offspring beamed in from different planets, the old and new worlds banging heads in the hope of getting some dizzy laughs.' Keith Watson, *Metro*.

Man Down

Greg Davies once again stars in this British comedy, *Man Down*. However, not only does he play the leading role in the show, he also created and wrote the sitcom, which is based on a man who hates his job as a teacher. The show aired in October 2013 and a second series is scheduled for a 2014 release. Alongside Greg Davies stars Rik Mayall (the British comedian most famous for *The Young Ones*, *Blackadder*, *The New Statesman* and *Bottom*) as the father of Dan (played by Davies).

In an interview with *British Comedy Guide*, Greg discusses casting Rik Mayall for the part of his dad:

It was easy in that I thought before I'd even started writing the sitcom, 'Wouldn't it be amazing if Rik Mayall was my dad because I've been compared to him for the last ten years and, of course, he's one of my comedy heroes.' It was a fantasy casting in my head before I'd even started writing it and then to find out he was interested was beyond exciting.

What They Said

Channel4.com asked Greg Davies if the role of Dan was in some ways autobiographical and based on his own life as a teacher:

I think it's hugely autobiographical yes because I was a very unhappy teacher for a long time – for 13 years – and I think I've mined that period which felt like a directionless period. I mean obviously I had an awful lot of fun and I hope that's where the fun in this show comes from watching a man disintegrate a little bit as a lot of us do in our lives at some point. 'Directionless' is the best way I can think to say it. That's what happens to this silly man who prioritises the wrong things so it's autobiographical in the sense that I did have a period where I was all over the place really. I didn't really get very far but you know I had a lot of fun!

Reviews

'I have to say *Man Down* was the biggest surprise of the Christmas season as I was expecting not to laugh at all while watching. It may well have been I'd had too much to eat and drink at this point, but I still found *Man Down* to be a comically surreal slice of festive fun.' Matt Donnelly, *The Custard TV*.

'The more it went on, the more we came to love Greg Davies's beautifully tasteless sitcom. His character Dan may be a towering oaf of a teacher who swears at pupils, insults his own parents and exploits his friends, but we still want things to go right for him.' David Butcher, *Radio Times*.

'We've seen Greg Davies play a teacher before, of course, and the workless, foul-mouthed truce struck between him and his flock here does smack a little of Jack Whitehall's *Bad Education*, but *Man Down*'s shortcomings in originality are nulled by a relentless volley of gags, all at Davies's expense, and with many arriving courtesy of a brilliantly cast Rik Mayall as his sadistic prankster dad. Crude, silly and very funny.' Luke Holland & Gwilym Mumford, *The Guardian*.

PhoneShop

PhoneShop was a Channel 4 sitcom that ran from 2010–13. The show featured Martin Trenaman, who played Simon's dad Alan Cooper in *The Inbetweeners*. Martin plays the character of Lance, the store manager of a fictional phone shop in London. The comedy was first commissioned in 2010 for six episodes and subsequently went on to air another two series, both of six episodes each.

PhoneShop was created and written by Phil Bowker, who is a British writer, producer and director whose list of credits include *The 11 O'Clock Show*, *Time Gentlemen Please* and *Pulling*.

What They Said

Martin Trenaman spoke to *British Comedy Guide* about how much influence they have on their character's development: 'Phil Bowker is the writer of the show and he produces, writes and directs it. We trust him implicitly. We do have an input but, ultimately, it is his decision as to what happens with the characters and where it goes. He is very happy for us to improvise but overall he is the Governor… in a very nice way.'

Although Martin's character is a phone-shop store manager, he admits to knowing nothing about mobile phones! 'I've gone into a shop and upgraded and they assume, hilariously, that you know everything about phones. They sort of get all this stuff out and say, yeah, this has Bluetooth, etc. etc. and you have to stop them and say, "Woah, woah, what is happening? What does that mean?" I'm still trying to work out Facetime on mine. I don't know what's going on.'

Writer Phil Bowker spoke to *Digital Spy* about mobile phones in general and his comedic response gives us an insight into the current technological world we live in: 'You get the train in to London on a morning and it's full of grown men playing video games. Mate, read a book! Improve yourself! Improve your life! It's ridiculous.'

Reviews

'This crass – and sometimes inspired – comedy commissioned for E4 is blessed by the presence of Emma Fryer. Her deluded mobile-phone saleswoman, Janine, is trying to climb the Croydon social ladder. Meanwhile, her equally deluded four male colleagues at the phone shop attempt to launch a series of calamitous sidelines, including an escort agency.' Ben Walsh, *The Independent on Sunday*.

'I love it, can you tell? It's puerile, yes, silly as silly. Nothing wrong with that; quite a lot right with that, actually. It's also brilliantly performed by Martin Trenaman and co, and brilliantly written and made by Phil Bowker.' Sam Wollaston, the *Guardian*.

'As usual with *PhoneShop*, plenty is made of a fairly skinny storyline. This is mainly thanks to the superb, intuitive and very funny cast. *PhoneShop* didn't seem like an obvious stayer when it started. But, as we begin the third series, it's proved to be a minor but surprisingly enduring pleasure.' Phil Harrison, *Time Out*.

The Impressions Show

The Impressions Show with Culshaw and Stephenson has been running for three series since 2009 and features main impressionist actors Jon Culshaw and Debra Stephenson. Belinda

Stewart-Wilson, aka Polly Mackenzie in *The Inbetweeners*, starred as Nigella Lawson in three episodes in the second series.

Throughout the show, Culshaw and Stephenson portrayed a range of celebrities such as Ross Kemp, Lord Alan Sugar, Davina McCall and Claudia Winkleman, to name a few. In early 2014 there were rumours of a fourth series. However, they were never confirmed.

Reviews

'It's rare to find impressionists whose material matches their talent but for most of this enjoyable half-hour programme Jon Culshaw and Debra Stephenson have pulled it off. Both find moments to shine.' Toby Antic, *The Daily Telegraph*.

'What happened to impressionists? There was a time when it was the blue-chip form of light entertainment, and no weekend or Christmas was complete without a special. But the steam seems to have gone out of it a little these days. *The Impressions Show* has its moments… but all too often if you close your eyes you wouldn't have a clue who was being lampooned. It gives an impression of being entertaining, but not always a convincing one.' Tom Sutcliffe, *The Independent*.

'Any sketch show is bound to be a hit or miss affair, but the celebrity parodies done by Jon Culshaw and Debra Stephenson are so amazingly accomplished, you can forgive the odd item that doesn't quite work.' Jane Rackham, *Radio Times*.

The Hour

The Hour is a BBC current-affairs drama set in the 1950s, with Dominic West (best known for playing Detective Jimmy McNulty in the HBO series *The Wire*) as the main star. The significance of *The Hour* is that it features Hannah Tointon in the second series. Hannah played Simon's love interest, Tara, in the third series of *The Inbetweeners*. Hannah plays the part of Kiki Delaine for six episodes of *The Hour*, which originally aired in 2012. There's more about Hannah in the section 'The Inbetweeners' Other Halves'.

The Hour only ran for two seasons and was axed by the BBC in 2013.

What They Said

Hannah told *Digital Spy* about her role of Kiki in the show: 'She's the showgirl. She's been brought up in this world – she doesn't really have any family and I think she's just in this horrible world. She's basically a prostitute but it's so undercover and weird – she sort of has this lifestyle that she's almost… kept.'

In the same interview, she also spoke of her role in *The Inbetweeners* and if she preferred comedy to drama: 'To be honest, I am somebody that as long as I have a character, it doesn't really matter if it's comedy or drama – I think timing is important in either. But for me, it's all about having a character to work on. I guess I find it all quite similar really.'

Reviews

'It was billed as Britain's answer to *Mad Men*, but *The Hour* does not have its American rival's longevity.' Daisy Wyatt, *The Independent*.

'Any period piece set in the 1950s is bound to look a lot like *Mad Men*, and this narrative also unfolds through an amber haze of cigarette smoke, whiskey and social taboos.' Alessandra Stanley, *nytimes.com*.

'*The Hour*, like *Mad Men*, is a slow burn, but in just six episodes, pulls in more social, cultural and political threads than a full season of *Mad Men*. That's not to say it's a better show, but it is perhaps more dense and ambitious.' Dustin Rowels, *pajiba.com*.

Plebs

Plebs is an ITV2 sitcom that premiered in 2013 for its first series and, in the same year, a second series was commissioned, due for release in 2014. The premise of the sitcom revolves around three men in Ancient Rome, whose only aim is to gain respect from the ladies and hold down good jobs!

Plebs stars Joel Fry (*White Van Man*), Tom Rosenthal (*Friday Night Dinner*) and Lydia Rose Bewley, who played Jane in *The Inbetweeners Movie*. Critics have made many comparisons between the series and the likes of *The Inbetweeners* and *Blackadder*, and in December 2013 *Plebs* won Best New Comedy at the British Comedy Awards.

What They Said

Lydia Rose Bewley spoke to *whatculture.com* about how she got the part of Medulla in the show *Plebs*:

I heard about *Plebs* a year ago, and really wanted to audition it. I got the audition whilst doing promotion for *The Inbetweeners Movie* in LA, so I had to send in a tape of me auditioning rather than go back to the UK to do it, and did it in a garage with two of my brothers. It went really well and a week later I started rehearsing for *Plebs*. I was thrilled because I really wanted that audition and had been going for it for ages.

Tom Rosenthal told *Digital Spy* about the idea of the show being set in Ancient Rome. 'I like the idea of a sitcom set in Ancient Rome – that period always makes you think of history lessons and classical themes and art history and all this, so the idea of sticking a sitcom there... I just quite liked that juxtaposition.'

Reviews

'Let's face it, it's not exactly a golden age for British sitcoms. So when a half-indecent one stumbles along, let's hope it's given time to grow.' Keith Watson, *Metro*.

'A playful disregard for historical accuracy and some strong comic turns, most notably from Ryan Sampson as dimwit slave Grunion, make Rome-com *Plebs* a more enjoyable watch than its ropey-looking trails suggest.' *The Guardian*.

'Not only will boys be boys but they always have been: that's the idea behind this comedy billed as *The Inbetweeners* meets Ancient Rome. Don't let that put you off. Yes, the gags are puerile, but you won't need to scrub yourself down in a cold shower afterwards.' Claire Webb, *Radio Times*.

Drifters

Dubbed as the female version of *The Inbetweeners*, *Drifters* centres around three young graduates living in Leeds and their strife when it comes to finding a job and a place to live. The show premiered on E4 in October 2013, with the first series ending in November of the same year. In early 2014 it was yet to be discussed whether *Drifters* would receive a second series.

Aside from the sitcom being likened to *The Inbetweeners*, the comedy connections go much further: three of the stars from *The Inbetweeners Movie* are the main characters. Jessica Knappett, who plays Meg in *Drifters* (and Lisa in *The Inbetweeners Movie*) not only stars in the show but also created and wrote all of the episodes in the first series; Lydia Rose Bewley (Jane in *The Inbetweeners Movie*) plays the part of Bunny; and Lauren O'Rourke (Nicole in *The Inbetweeners Movie*) plays Laura. Lauren and Jessica first knew of each other through the comedy live circuit and, when they hooked up with Lydia on the set of *The Inbetweeners Movie*, the chemistry was set in stone.

In addition, Damon Beesley and Iain Morris (creators of *The Inbetweeners*) were executive producers on the show and, in an interview in 2013 with *comedy.co.uk*, Jessica Knappett had this to say about the comedy pair: 'They are teenagers trapped in grown men's bodies. I loved it. They're the best teachers I've ever had AND they always pay for lunch.' Nice to see Iain and Damon giving back a little something after the huge success of *The Inbetweeners*!

What They Said

Jessica Knappett spoke to *British Comedy Guide* about how much of the series is based on her real life:

> Tragically quite a lot of it is loosely based on real life. There's one episode that is almost entirely true, based on real events but rearranged into a different order – I'm not going to say which episode! After it all happened to me in real life, I told my friend the story and she said I couldn't put it in *Drifters* because 'nobody would believe it'.

Jessica also spoke to *spindlemagazine.com* about the comparisons to *The Inbetweeners*:

I didn't think in a million years they would let me and Lydia be in a show together, just because of the closeness to *The Inbetweeners*, thinking 'oh no that's just going to look like it's a spin-off', which of course it isn't because we're playing completely different characters. I saw loads and loads of people for the part [of Bunny], but when Lydia came in she was just hands down the funniest person, there was no arguing with it. But after a while you forget [the connection], [*Drifters*] is just so different.'

As *Drifters* is basically all about not knowing what to do with your life after university, Jessica gives her top tips on how to become a drifter:

1. Make sure you do everything you possibly can to keep running from your future/major life/career decisions. Ideally, this should involve taking out a loan and travelling to another continent to spend it there.

2. When someone asks you what you're up to, simply reply, 'I've just got back from India,' for at least nine months after your return.

3. 'Going to India again' is a perfectly acceptable response to questions about future plans. Ignore your dad when he tells you that 'going to a country is not the same as having an aim in life'.

4. Never underestimate Facebook as the best way to break up with someone.

5. Living at your mum and dad's at the age of 24 isn't 'sad' or 'immature', it makes total business sense! Unless they charge you rent to teach you a 'valuable lesson' about growing up.

6. Make sure you get a job you don't care about just to pay

your rent. The more demoralising, underpaid and humiliating the better.

7. Do think twice if someone offers you a modelling job in a vodka bar in Leeds.

8. At some point, you will need to teach your ex-boyfriend the difference between you playing hard to get and you having absolutely no interest in him anymore.

9. When trying to ditch the ex, arm yourself with some useful metaphors, like comparing him to famous serial killers. Then, maybe, move back in with him.

10. Being a drifter is all about making terrible life choices, after all.

Reviews

'E4 was aiming for the new *Inbetweeners* but ended up with the new *Coming of Age* – *Drifters* was one of the worst comedies of any year. Cartoon characters, gags that ranged from the mind-numbingly obvious – adults acting like teenagers – to the offensive – depression played for laughs – and a truly bizarre lead performance from a wide-eyed Jessica Knappett, gurning her way through all 138 painful minutes.' Morgan Jeffery, *Digital Spy*.

'*Drifters* was definitely at its strongest when it was focusing on the banter between the three girls, played by three actresses with superb comic timing. The themes in the programme will resonate with everyone who's struggled to know what to do with their lives after they've left university.' *The Custard TV*.

'The characters are unbelievable, a fact emphasised by the flimsy storyline and a serious lack of witticisms for a so-called comedy. It's hard to accept there's a place where the inhabitants resemble *Drifters* but, if there is, it's not one that should be used for entertainment purposes. Ever.' Danielle Goldstein, *Time Out*.

The Musketeers

The Musketeers was BBC1's flagship series in January 2014: a historical drama based on the famous characters of Alexandre Dumas's *The Three Musketeers*. The show was written by British writer and producer Adrian Hodges, whose credits include *Rome*, *Primeval* and the 2011 film *My Week with Marilyn*.

Tamla Kari (of *The Inbetweeners Movie* and *Cuckoo* fame) plays the part of Constance Bonacieux, a young married woman who is an acquaintance of the Musketeers.

What They Said

Tamla told the BBC about her character Constance:

> Constance Bonacieux is the young wife of the town's cloth merchant. Her life is comfortable but void of excitement and happiness. She becomes involved with the Musketeers and this all changes. You see the true Constance. She's feisty, intelligent and passionate. She really holds her own against the boys and you wouldn't mess with her. Despite all this, underneath there's a massive vulnerability. She has a beautiful soul and is completely selfless.

Reviews

'I tried very hard on three separate occasions to enjoy BBC1's new much heralded buckle of swash *The Musketeers*. And by the third attempt realised I'd written one note on my pad which said, "Musketeers? Bored to tears, more like! AM I RIGHT?", which is neither a terribly pithy joke or particularly constructive smite, but was simply all I could muster.' Grace Dent, *The Independent*.

'We're not bothering with *Call the Midwife* today – too dreary. Don't call her. Or *Mr Selfridge* – who cares? I'm seeking adventure, romance, the buckling of swash. Found it! In *The Musketeers*.' Sam Woolaston, *The Guardian*.

'A slick, whirlwind adventure, *The Musketeers* is essentially old-fashioned fare with a fresh lick of paint, but there's absolutely nothing wrong with that.' Morgan Jeffrey, *Digital Spy*.

Edge of Heaven

Edge of Heaven is an ITV comedy drama about a 1980s-themed guest house in Margate. The show starred Blake Harrison as Alfie, a loser in love whose fiancée left him at the altar. The show also stars Camille Coduri (best known for playing Jackie Tyler in *Doctor Who*) and Nitin Kundra (a British actor who has made several appearances in classic shows, such as *Emmerdale*, *Casualty* and *Silent Witness* – he is also famous for playing the recurring character Indian Kieth in the ITV2 comedy panel show *Celebrity Juice*). *Edge of Heaven* aired in February 2014 as a six-part series.

What They Said

In an interview with *British Comedy Guide*, Blake spoke about his character Alfie and if there were any resemblances to himself:

This is the closest character wise I have played to myself really. I have been heartbroken and upset before and so it is stuff I can totally relate to. I have got an understanding of him and that's been really nice.

When I played Neil in *The Inbetweeners*, I had to work out why someone that dumb would come out with his logic, but with Alfie I do feel sorry for him. I hope viewers do warm to him and I hope they will want him to be happy.

Reviews

'ITV's new comedy drama often resembled a smoking wreckage, but there was something unexpectedly likable about the ragamuffin characters.' Ed Power, *The Daily Telegraph*.

'Here's a sample gag from *Edge of Heaven*: "I'm like those birds that go around in pairs." "Lesbians?" "No, swans." If you're laughing so hard you've bent double and displaced a vertebra in your back, then this broad, camp comedy drama is for you.' Alison Graham, *Radio Times*.

'*Edge of Heaven* is loud, colourful and brilliantly character driven [which] means you're bound to find at least one character to fall in love with. And if you happen to be out on a Friday night, it's the perfect show to nurse that Saturday-morning hangover too!' Elliot Gonzalez, *I Talk Telly*.

The American Inbetweeners

In 2012 an American version of *The Inbetweeners* was made and broadcast on MTV. Writers of the UK show Damon Beesley and Iain Morris worked as executive producers on the US version, which was developed by Brad Copeland, an American writer and producer who is best known for his work on *Arrested Development* and *My Name is Earl*.

Premiering in August 2012, the show ran for 12 episodes in total. In November 2012 MTV announced that they were to cancel the production due to low ratings. Many of the storylines were adaptations of those in the UK version but with an American twist for the benefit of the viewer – for example, the famous 'bus wankers!' scene, where the lads shout out of the car window to people waiting at a bus stop, was subsequently changed in the US remake to the line 'bus turds!' However, there were a lot of aspects of the show that remained the same – in particular, all of the main characters' names. Many British fans of the UK programme have been extremely disappointed with the show, with a lot of newspapers at the time calling it a 'flop'. MTV, when they made the announcement about the programme's cancellation, said, 'While we won't be moving forward with another season of *The Inbetweeners*, we enjoyed working with the show's creators and such a talented, funny cast.'

It's pretty clear that the show didn't have the same impact 'across the pond' as it did in the UK, as not one of the 12 episodes made it past a million viewers in America. We think that a lot of the storylines and jokes in the UK version are very much aligned to a British audience and wouldn't have had the same resonance elsewhere. Much of the vernacular in the show is not really suited to an American audience, which is why it didn't really take off as it did here. That's not to say that a remake wouldn't be successful but possibly that the series tried to be *too* much like the original, rather than forging its own path to suit the viewer.

Aside from the poor ratings, MTV was right, there was an incredibly talented cast on the show. Here we'll take a look at the main actors in the US version – they are part of *The Inbetweeners'* legacy in their own right!

Joey Pollari

Joey, who plays the part of Will Mackenzie in the show, was born on 9 April 1994 in Minnesota. Before playing Will, he was best known for playing the part of Tyler Burns in the Disney TV movie *Skyrunners*, an American sci-fi thriller that sees Tyler gain superhuman abilities when a UFO crashes near his town. It was a role that won Joey a Young Artist Award for Leading Young Actor.

Bubba Lewis

Before playing Simon Cooper, Bubba Lewis played a number of roles within US television, many of which made it big in the UK. His first major role was in the war film *Flags of Our Fathers*, a production directed by Clint Eastwood and starring Ryan Phillippe. He then went on to have small acting roles in the famous US drama series *ER*, *Grey's Anatomy* and *Dexter*, along with children's TV series *Hannah Montana*. When finding out he had the chance to audition for the part of Simon Cooper, Bubba told *huffingtonpost.com* how he was, naturally, excited: 'It was so crazy because I fell in love with Simon first, because that's who I related with the most. I'm such a huge fan of the original. That's why when I found out, I was instantly like, "I have to read for this somehow".'

Zack Pearlman

Born in Michigan in May 1988, Zack plays the part of Jay Cartwright in the US version of *The Inbetweeners*. Zack made a name for himself in the 2010 film *The Virginity Hit*, a comedy produced by Will Ferrell about a group of friends who buy a bong but vow not to use it until one of them loses their virginity.

Zack's other main role came as a voice on the Dreamworks animated TV series *Dragons: Riders of Berk*, where he voiced the character of Snotlout for 38 out of the 40 episodes that have run so far. A third season of the show is expected to be released at some point in 2014.

Mark L. Young

Mark, who plays the part of Neil Sutherland, was born in Washington in 1991. Before gaining the part in *The Inbetweeners*, he plied his trade from the age of around 12 in some of America's most famous and influential TV shows, including *Six Feet Under*, *The O.C.*, *CSI: Crime Scene Investigation* and *Cold Case*. By the time he was 15, he had established himself as a credible actor and made appearances in more *CSI* and other shows, such as *ER* and *Dexter*. In 2013, Mark played the role of Scottie in the film *We're the Millers*, alongside Jason Sudeikis and Jennifer Aniston. It's a film about a drug dealer who stitches together a make-believe family in order to smuggle marijuana across the Mexican border.

Alex Frnka

Alex plays the part of Carli D'Amato. Before clinching the part, she had played small roles in the American TV series *I'm in the Band* and the TV movie *Unanswered Prayers*. When she got the part in *The Inbetweeners*, she admitted to *huffingtonpost.com* that she hadn't seen the original.

> Once I got the audition my manager was like, 'Oh, it's a remake of this great, famous UK series,' I was like, 'I don't want to watch it now. I want to wait until after.' So after we

filmed our season, I sat down and watched them all and got to see the movie with Iain [Morris]. I loved it. I was able to appreciate them both on two different levels.

Brett Gelman

America's very own Mr Gilbert is played by actor, writer, producer and director Brett Gelman. Brett has starred in a number of famous American sitcoms, such as *Curb Your Enthusiasm* and *The Office*. He also featured in the 2010 film *The Other Guys*, starring Mark Wahlberg and Will Ferrell.

Even after the cancellation of the series, there has been talk of making an adaptation of *The Inbetweeners Movie* in the US and in August 2013 it was rumoured that Jim Field Smith (an English director, writer and producer) would be directing the film with the working title *Virgins America*.

Reviews

So *The Inbetweeners* remake in America didn't go down well with the critics but why? Let's take a look at what they said about the show:

'After watching three episodes of the US version on MTV, I'm not sure I can reassure anyone that *The Inbetweeners* isn't as bad as feared. The early shows barely raised a smile, let alone reached the comedic heights achieved by the Channel 4 version. Because of the show's huge popularity in the UK, the last thing I'd imagine the creators want is a direct comparison with the British version. But given that the initial episodes follow, almost scene for scene and sometimes word for word, the British script, it is impossible not to compare.' Mark Hughes, the *Independent*.

'The problem with MTV's *Inbetweeners* isn't that it's bad, just

The lads found a few things to laugh at along the way on Comic Relief's Rude Road Trip.

©*Rex Features*

Above: Joe Thomas, Simon Bird, Blake Harrison and James Buckley (left to right) attend a private screening of *I Love You, Man* in 2009.

Below: The gang head out to the BAFTA After Party in 2010 to celebrate picking up the *Radio Times* Audience Award.

Above: The boys are joined by their fellow cast members Hannah Tointon, Belinda Stewart-Wilson and Emily Head (left to right) at the National Television Awards in 2011.

Below: The girls of *The Inbetweeners Movie* enjoy a taste of the red carpet at the premiere.

Above left: Mr Gilbert, played by Greg Davies, was one of our favourite characters on the show.

Above right: The boys all loved Will's mum, played by Belinda Stewart-Wilson, for obvious reasons.

Below left: Emily Atack, who played Charlotte 'Big Jugs' Hinchcliffe, with Simon Bird – looking slightly less awkward with her than he does on the show.

Below right: Emily Head, Joe Thomas and Hannah Tointon (left to right) at the *Inbetweeners Movie* premiere afterparty.

Above: The lads enjoyed their moment on the red carpet at the premiere to their first movie.

Below: Laura Haddock, Jessica Knappet, Tamla Kari and Lydia Rose Bewley (left to right) played the love interests in the movie.

Above left: Blake Harrison and 'The Ginger', his long-term girlfriend Kerry-Ann Lynch.

Above right: It comes as a shock to most, but James Buckley is actually married with two kids!

Below: The boys have all gone on to exciting new projects since *The Inbetweeners* finished. James Buckley starred alongside Shia LaBeouf in *The Necessary Death of Charlie Countryman*.

Above left: The Harry Hill Movie wasn't quite the box office success that was hoped, but Simon Bird played his part of a vet very well. © *Rex Features*

Above right: Simon Bird with his co-stars Tom Rosenthal and Tamsin Greig from the well-received comedy *Friday Night Dinner*. © *Rex Features*

Below left: Joe Thomas has had better luck than his character Simon with Hannah Tointon, and they have been dating ever since meeting on set.

Below right: One of the most successful comedies on TV at the moment, *Fresh Meat*, stars Joe Thomas alongside a very strong cast.

The gang return to the big screen in
August 2014 for the next instalment of
Britain's favourite comedy

All Pictures © Getty Images unless otherwise stated

that it offers nothing unique for the culture that spawned what the UK show subverted.' Dan Owen, *MSN TV*.

'Only reinforcing the old stereotype, the American producers have misunderstood how the humour in the series worked, and focused on bringing out the wrong parts for its conversion, leaving us with a shadow of the original, albeit a just about competent one. Maybe if I didn't love the original series as much as I do, I would perhaps pass this programme as average. But considering the material they had to work with, it is very disappointing indeed. Now let's pray that this adaptation of *The Inbetweeners Movie* they have been discussing does not see the light of day…' Richard Priday, *theyorker.co.uk*.

CHAPTER FIVE

THE INBETWEENERS MOVIE

INTRODUCTION

Love the first film? Of course you did. Well here's a recap of all the best bits broken down into bite-size chunks so you can find all of your favourite moments.

The Pussay Patrol

The movie starts with Will visiting his dad (played by actor Anthony Head of the Nescafé Gold Blend commercial and *Buffy the Vampire Slayer* fame). Just like Polly McKenzie, Will's father knows his son is a bit of an oddball; so much so that he didn't even invite his son to his 'remarriage' to Suzanne, the work-experience girl he left Polly for:

'I was going to invite you but I know how you are around people… awkward, weird.' After all, it was only a couple of hundred close friends and family who were invited! So when he finds out that Will is off for a summer holiday he's not expecting his son to go on the usual lads' holiday, like Magaluf, Ibiza or Zante. Instead, he imagines that Will is going to do something a little less ordinary ('Tran Siberian Express, fossil hunting in Dorset…') but Will insists he's going somewhere normal with his normal friends (if you can call Jay, Simon and Neil normal!).

So it's the summer and the lads are all doing their thing. Jay is enjoying some alone time with some swimming goggles, a snorkel, a packet of ham and a live stream of an Eastern European woman, Neil is working hard (well, working) on a fish counter at the local supermarket and Simon has been spending time with the love of his life, Carli D'Amato, who he's been chasing for literally years. But things are all about to change…

Jay's mum walks in on him as he's halfway through a packet of ham (not eating it) to break the news that his granddad has died, Carli breaks things off with Simon because they're both off to uni after summer and she wants to enjoy a holiday as a singleton beforehand, and it's the last day of school for all four of the lads.

So to help Simon get over Carli and to give Jay a chance to spend his inheritance money, the gang decide to get away from it all on what Jay describes as 'two weeks of sun, sea, sex, sand, booze, sex, minge, fanny and tits and booze and sex'. And with Neil agreeing that 'they say the summer is the perfect time to go on a summer holiday', they jet off for a fortnight in Malia, holiday 'Pussay Patrol' T-shirts at the ready: Jay 'Mr Big Nob', Simon 'Mr Rebound', Neil 'Mr Ladykiller' and, last but not least in inappropriateness, Will 'Mr I fuck kids'.

When the lads arrive at the airport, Will has the itinerary all planned out: 'Get to the apartment, unpack, get some sleep and head out fresh tomorrow. First stop, the Minoan Palace at

Knossos.' But Jay has a slightly different idea and is pretty vocal in telling this to Will:

'We haven't come halfway around the world to look at some boring fucking Greek ruins… we get there, drop the bags off and then go straight out and get spazticated. Simples.'

And as they arrive at the hotel, which looks more like a Chernobyl fallout shelter than a Greek resort, they're told by the manager (who is just finishing pulling a dead dog from a well outside) to have fun but that there's a €50 fine each time they shit on the floor. Classy establishment!

The lads don't let things get them too down though, apart from Will, who is told he has to sleep in the bath, and after a touch of male grooming and a few sprays of Lynx, the lads head out to enjoy their first night of Malia nightlife because, in Jay's words, 'the gash isn't gonna fuck itself'.

Did You Know?
The hotel the lads stay in during the film is actually the derelict Hotel Rocamar in Soller Port, Majorca. In fact, much of the film was filmed in Majorca between February and April – mainly in clubbing capital Magaluf. It's rumoured the film's producers chose to shoot in Magaluf instead of Malia where the film was set because it would be easier to find out-of-season workers available to be extras on the Spanish island.

The First Night
As they hit the main strip, Jay and Neil are in awe. Scantily clad girls as far as the eye can see and plenty of drinks flowing. After a bit of an explore, they're approached by a PR girl from 'Marco's', which, in her words, has a 'really chilled out and sexy

vibe'. So after the offer of some cheap shots and Jay thinking he's in there with the PR girl, the lads head in only to be hit with a completely empty club. But undeterred, the lads get stuck in and order the first round: four pints, four fish bowls and a Jägermeister. It's going to get messy!

Shockingly, before they even finish their first round, other people actually enter the club and this time it's four girls! Jay decides he's going to sit it out and wait for the PR girl to make an appearance but isn't short of handing out some advice to the others as they argue about who should walk over and make the first move: 'You don't just walk over and introduce yourselves. It's creepy. You dance over near them, make the eyes and get them to dance over with ya.'

For the first time ever, Simon actually agrees with something that's come out of Jay's mouth and movie brilliance follows.

'We No Speak Americano' by Yolanda Be Cool & DCUP hits the speakers and Will, Neil and Simon dance over. Neil starts the gang off with a bit of robot, Simon with some on-the-spot shaking and Will opts for a horse-trot-like move! The 'routine' finishes with the three dancing in sync-ish.

Unbelievably, after a bit of pleading from Will, the lads are given the OK to sit with the girls but the banter doesn't really flow too well with Lucy, Alison, Jane and Lisa. Will makes a start by offending Alison with sarcastic remarks about her barman Greek lover Nicos, Jay completely ignores Jane, instead opting to rob drinks from behind the bar, and Simon starts to go into great detail with Lucy about how great Carli is and how much he loves her. Smooth guys.

After a quiet start, Neil looks like he's going to be a bit more successful than the others (despite the fact that he has a girlfriend back home) and he manages to get Lisa onto the dance floor to showcase some more of his signature moves. However, it quickly goes downhill when he leaves her to dance with some larger ladies in their 40s or 50s – hard to tell really with all the make-up! So on that note, the girls decide to call it a night, with the surprising suggestion to the lads that they meet up some time – maybe at the all-day boat party that Friday.

As the boys decide to leave, Simon, for the umpteenth time, thinks he's spotted love-of-his-life Carli on the strip – only this time he's actually right! Thinking it's a sign from greater powers that him and Carli should be together, Neil goes on to explain that, in fact, he just asked Carli where her and her mates were off for the summer because they were cooler than the guys. This pisses Simon off for a few seconds because Neil knew he'd come to help get over Carli but this quickly passes when he finds out that she'll be at the boat party. Now he knows he definitely wants to try to get tickets.

So off home a now cheery Simon goes (despite being a little bit run over by a PR guy Carli seems very friendly with), with Will closely following behind. Neil returns to the club to continue 'finger-banging' one of the older ladies he's met and Jay wanders off down the road for more booze and birds.

The next morning starts with as much drama as the night before. Back in the run-down hotel Simon and Will are awoken by something that 'sounded like Big-foot having an asthma attack', which turns out to be Neil and the dinner lady he met the night before. They appear to be having a good time though as she calls out: 'Spunk all over me bastard tits. Bite it, spit on it, twist it right fucking hard.' Anyway, after the 'love-making' is over, the lads decide to head over to the hotel where the girls from the previous night are staying to try to get some boat-party tickets for Friday. So they pick Jay up from the floor outside, where he'd slept face-down in an ants' nest, and head off to the resort.

Little Weenie

When the boys arrive at the girls' hotel, it's quickly apparent that holiday bookings should never be left to Neil. Compared to the lads' gaff it's palatial and the four decide to bed down and catch a few rays.

Jay doesn't let the little fact that there's no loungers available spoil his sunning. Deciding the towels left on a group of beds are probably just down to some Germans who've got up early, he launches them into the pool and begins to relax, despite Simon's protests: 'That towel's got *Finding Nemo* on it.' 'What, so Nazis can't like Disney too?'

After accepting the fact that they can enjoy the sun in the beds Jay has found them, Simon goes on to draw a cock on Will's back using sun cream and Jay and Neil go to check out the 'chicas' around the pool. They actually seem to be getting the right sort of attention from the ladies when a little kid runs over to the pair and starts playing around with them. Jay keeps him amused in an attempt to show his caring side to the nearby girls but what he doesn't anticipate is the kid then deciding to push him into the pool, trainers and all! Everyone around the pool bursts out laughing and it hasn't done Jay's attempts to pull any favours but he takes Neil's advice and leaves the kid alone, laughing the embarrassing incident off.

After the laughter has died down, the four girls from Marco's turn up. Again, Simon seems to be hitting it off with Lucy and Will with Alison (although she still has a Greek boyfriend at this point).

When the conversation between Will and Alison turns to sex, virgin Will starts getting very awkward but he graphically admits, 'I have never put my penis in a lady,' and she seems fine with that. Things get worse for Simon though, as he again blows his chances with Lucy. She gets excited when he confirms that they want to join the girls on the forthcoming boat party but this quickly turns into annoyance as he explains that Carli is going to be there and that's why he's going.

After a few more embarrassing moments with the girls, the gang get into a spot of bother as the family who were using the loungers before them returns. While an argument kicks off between the dad and Will, who realises the girl in the family is disabled and that's why there's so much uproar, Jay's little mate from before returns.

He gets the better of Jay for the second time, not throwing him into the pool again but pulling down his shorts in front of everyone to reveal Jay's penis! 'So little, so little,' the kid shouts and, to get him back, Jay launches him into the pool. The poor kid can't swim though and, after being rescued by a couple of other holidaymakers, the gang are kicked out of the hotel. Things then go from bad to worse as Simon realises he has now missed out on his chance to get boat-party tickets and, after blaming Jay, the pair get involved in some fisticuffs that have to get broken up by the other boys.

So for a while the boys go their separate ways. After Jay shows Neil that he'd actually already bought the four tickets for the boat party and goes on to rip them up in anger, they head out for another 'Pussay Patrol'.

Meanwhile, Simon hatches a 'brilliant' plan to raise enough funds for a boat-party ticket of his own, to finally get his chance to win Carli back: sell his clothes! Yes, that's right, he and Will head off to stand with the 'lucky lucky' men.

He's not having much luck selling his gear, or maybe he is, depending on how you see things. But after a while he's approached by rep James and his mates, who come up with some obviously made-up story that his mate has had his apartment broken into and all of his clothes nicked. He offers to buy all of Simon's stuff (including everything he's wearing) for €100 and, after stupidly agreeing, Si strips off and waits for James to return with the cash. Obviously, he doesn't.

Things don't go as planned for Jay and Neil either. They somehow end up in a club watching a show where a man pleasures himself, then, after trying to befriend the same rep James, end up almost in tears after the idiot PR guy strangles Jay.

So the four end up back where it all began – Marco's Club – and after a few cross words, Jay offers to buy the lads the drinks as they're all out of cash. After a fish bowl and a few suicide shots, the lads are all best mates again, having a great laugh!

Unbelievably, the boys bump into the girls again and, after Alison makes a pact with Will that she'll sleep with him if he's still a virgin a year later, and Lisa leaves Neil for motor-boating another older lady, they all head down to the beach for a midnight swim.

Again though, the lads manage to blow it. Jay turns down Jane's advances because he's embarrassed in front of other people (even though he clearly still likes her), Simon spots Carli on the beach and leaves Lucy alone in the sea, and Will tops it off by losing his glasses and stumbling into Alison's boyfriend Nicos with another woman, all this after taking his clothes off!

So the lads have messed up again. But after the wisest words ever spoken by Neil (OK so maybe not the first bit) – 'I stopped believing in God when I realised it was just dog backwards and after that I just stopped worrying about stuff. You only get one go round I reckon and when you're dead, you're dead, so you can spend your time thinking about how things haven't went perfect or you can just get on with it, have a laugh and that...' – the lads decide to head out on the town and get 'royally fucked up on Jay's dead granddad's money'. After a night of midgets, dancing, quad-biking, upside-down drinking, kebabs and vomiting, the lads have finally had the hours of fun they wanted.

The Boat Party

The big day finally arrives. With Simon and Will without a ticket, the other two lads are all geared up for sun, booze and possibly a bit of sex at the event the whole of Malia has been talking about. Lucy is still pissed-off with Simon for constantly going on about Carli and Alison still hasn't forgiven the very hungover Will for acting like a bit of a dick about Nicos, but out of the blue she offers him a spare ticket and he obviously jumps at the chance, as his luck finally might be in!

So Simon, now on his own, finally realises he's been a bit of an idiot and apologises to Lucy, who clearly still likes him. So much so that she offers him her own ticket for the boat party. Still being a dick, Simon doesn't read between the lines and realise that this is his chance to win Lucy over, snatches the ticket out of her hand quicker than you can say '£1 tub of gel' and runs off for the boat!

On-board it's everything the guys expected and more. Music, drinks and plenty of girls. After the first round of shots is downed, Simon heads off to once again pursue Carli, Jay goes to find Jane for a dance, Will throws up on two unsuspecting couples and Neil is, well, just Neil and gets on with having a dance.

Things start to look up for the boys. Jay finds Jane and runs off to the toilet on the promise of a snog and a blow-job, Will receives the very, very surprising offer of a relationship with the gorgeous Alison and Lisa grabs Neil for the dry-hump she's been waiting for all holiday. Things are a little bit more complicated for Simon though. He finally gets hold of Carli who, in a complete shock, starts eating his face off but it's only then that he realises she's doing it to get the attention of club promoter James and he FINALLY realises he's made a mistake and Lucy is the one he should be chasing.

Simon then decides only a grand gesture is going to win her back. He goes on to climb on to the top of the boat and jump into the sea to swim to Lucy back on shore. It doesn't go quite to plan and he ends up being airlifted out of the water just a few metres from the boat but, when he gets back to dry land, the gesture seems to have paid off and all is forgiven with Lucy.

Simon gets out of hospital and, when the holiday is over, the guys and girls head back to the UK together leaving us all wanting more!

GIRLS FROM THE FIRST FILM

The boys were fantastic in the first movie but we've also got to take our hats off to the four love interests of the film, Lydia

Rose Bewley (Jane), Laura Haddock (Alison), Tamla Kari (Lucy) and Jessica Knappett (Lisa), because somehow they managed to take a bit of a liking to the Inbetweeners and made their trip to Malia epic!

Find out here where each of these talented actresses started out, how they got their shot to star in the first movie and what they've been up to since filming stopped.

Lydia Rose Bewley

Bewley played Jay's soon-to-be girlfriend in the first movie. The actress comes from a stage background, daughter of a professional opera singer, and younger sister to Charlie Bewley, who you'll probably better know as vampire Demetri in *The Twilight Saga* trilogy.

After graduating from the Oxford School of Drama in 2007, Bewley sweated it out as a children's entertainer before landing her big role in *The Inbetweeners Movie*. Bewley told the *Daily Mail* how much of a shock securing the role was: 'My former agent called me at a point where the acting was definitely drying up a bit, and he put me up for the role. It was a dream, especially as so many of my friends and acquaintances had also auditioned for it.'

Since her big break, Bewley has starred as sarcastic-slave Medulla in ITV2's Ancient Roman comedy hit *Plebs* and in E4 sitcom *Drifters*, where she plays Bunny, a young girl who's just returned from India, eccentric and up for giving anything a go.

And the talented young actress doesn't want to stop there, telling the *Daily Mail*: 'My dream would be to be told I'm doing a Jane Austen or Aphra Behn adaptation and I have to learn how to horse ride and fence.'

We reckon she'd be a lively addition to any period drama and would most definitely liven things up with her great personality, even admitting herself that 'I think I was born in the wrong era'.

Laura Haddock

Laura too started early when it came to performing. She told the *Daily Mail* how, despite not coming from a background in the arts, she knew at an early age that the stage was where she wanted to be:

> I remember being about eight and watching Pollyanna with Hayley Mills. I looked at my mum and said, 'Mum, I want to be Pollyanna.' She said, 'You're going to have to make yourself cry if you want to be an actress.' So I turned my head away, and when I turned it back I was in floods of tears. And mum was like, 'Oh God. That's it. We've lost her.'

And at just seventeen, she left school and moved to London to study drama at the Arts Educational School, getting her first TV break at 23 when she appeared in *Plus One* as part of Channel 4's *Comedy Showcase*.

A more experienced actress than the other girls in the film, Haddock had been involved in a number of TV and film projects before *The Inbetweeners Movie*, including starring as sexually confident P.A. Natasha in ITV comedy drama *Monday Monday*, and university student and love interest Samantha in BBC3 sitcom *How Not to Live Your Life*.

But despite all of this experience, getting the part in the movie was no easy job and, in fact, it was a close call for Haddock, who was initially rejected for the role for not being young enough. It was only after almost five months of recalls that the talented actress got the part and even then she had no idea just how big the movie would become, telling the *Daily Mail*, 'I thought the film would be a modest little British comedy that the fans would come to see. We went into it with that sort of giddy spirit.'

Since *The Inbetweeners Movie*, Laura has had a main role in British horror film *Storage 24*, playing the character of Nikki who, along with a group of six others, is trapped in a London storage facility with a mysterious creature that escaped from a military plane during a crash.

Laura also bagged a supporting role in 2014 movie *Guardians of the Galaxy*, based on the Marvel Comics superhero team. This is her first step into Hollywood and, working alongside big names including Bradley Cooper, Vin Diesel and Zoe Saldána, it's sure to provide the young actress with fantastic experience.

Even with her movie career well underway, the talented actress has still picked up big roles in small-screen work too, appearing in the second series of hit BBC1 drama *Upstairs Downstairs* as maid Beryl Ballard and in the award-winning American drama *Da Vinci's Demons* as Lucrezia Donati, the lover of Leonardo da Vinci: a bit different from Inbetweener Will!

Tamla Kari

Tamla (Simon's EVENTUAL love interest Lucy in the first movie) was the least experienced actress out of all the girls. Tamla was an A-class student, graduating from the Drama Centre London in 2011 with a First BA in Acting. There wasn't much time for Tamla to hone her skills though after finishing her studies and, in fact, landing *The Inbetweeners Movie* was actually her first role, as she explained to the *Daily Mail*:

> It's actually my first acting job, full stop. I got it when I was still at drama school, at the Drama Centre London. They allowed me to take my second term out to do the filming, so essentially the movie constituted my end-of-term project. I couldn't have asked for anything better. I was a huge fan of the show, so when I went for my audition, and Joe Thomas was sitting there, I tried to pretend I was cool, but I was so nervous.

You wouldn't believe watching the movie that this was Tamla's first role, as she is so convincing as Lucy and brilliant at putting Inbetweener Simon in his place on several occasions. But despite this being her first job, she explained how there was still plenty of time to have fun on set. 'We all kept referring to it as a holiday. Then we had to remind ourselves that no, actually, it's a really important job. But it was hard to keep that in mind at times. We went out to dinner together, us four girls, and hung out, and had a ball.'

And since the movie, Tamla's career has really taken off. After smaller roles in the BBC3 supernatural comedy drama *Being Human* and BBC1 drama *Silk*, Tamla got her next big break in *Cuckoo*. Tamla took a main role in the BBC3 sitcom mentioned earlier, which launched in 2012, where she played Rachel Thompson, a young girl who returns home after a year travelling with a bit of extra baggage – a man by the name of Cuckoo who she's married!

Cuckoo is played by American Emmy and Golden Globe-winning actor Andy Samberg, best known for his lead role in sitcom *Brooklyn Nine-Nine*, with other famous faces including *Inbetweeners* star Greg (Mr Gilbert) Davies and Helen Baxendale (Emily in *Friends*).

The young actress also appeared in ITV sitcom *The Job Lot*, set in a West Midlands job centre, and in BBC historical drama *The Musketeers* as Constance Bonacieux. With just a few years' acting under her belt, a hit movie and several key roles in TV, it looks like Tamla is already on the way to the top with her fellow *Inbetweeners* girls and boys.

Jessica Knappett

Last but by no means least of the *Inbetweeners* girls is Jessica Knappett, who played Neil's love interest in the first movie, Lisa. Well, besides his girlfriend and the couple of older women he befriends!

Like the others, Jessica studied the arts, opting for drama and english at university. When Jessica was at uni, she co-founded the sketch group Lady Garden, performing at the 2008 Edinburgh Fringe Festival as well as at other comedy festivals around the country.

But even with this experience, getting the role of Lisa in *The Inbetweeners Movie* came as a bit of a shock for Jessica, who told the *Daily Mail*:

> I'd been training with a catering company, and was going to become a catering assistant. I mean, acting was my primary thing, but I needed to pay the rent. But I did the read-through, they told me I'd got the part on the spot, and I started rehearsing an hour later. So I had to call the

catering company and say, 'Sorry, I'm in this movie. But, you know what? Let's leave the position open if we can.'

Since then though, work has been regular for the talented young actress and comedy writer, with appearances in E4's *Meet the Parents*, BBC's *How Not to Live Your Life* and *Lunch Monkey*.

But her most important achievement since finishing the movie is her work as a writer, alongside *Inbetweeners* wordsmiths Iain Morris and Damon Beesley. Together the trio co-write E4's smash-hit sitcom *Drifters*, with Jessica also starring in the show alongside Lydia Rose Bewley and one of Inbetweener Neil's other love conquests, Lauren O'Rourke (Nicole).

So between them, the girls of the first film have given the boys a run for their money, each doing exceptionally well since filming finished. That's no surprise, of course, as they were each absolutely brilliant in the movie and we can't wait to see what they pop up in next!

INBETWEENERS HOLIDAY GUIDE

Planning a holiday with some mates? In this section you can learn everything you need to know from the first movie to enjoy your fun in the sun:

Chicas

Good-looking girls lounging around the pool. The best way to impress is to walk past very slowly in your shorts and trainers (no top, obviously). But remember not to get pushed into the water by a little kid!

Children's Toilet

More commonly known as a bidet, this is a small porcelain loo in continental bathrooms with a tap so that, according to Jay, 'parents can check their kid's shit'. Beware though, if you do decide to take a dump in this undersized bog – missing the bowl and getting the floor could result in a €50 fine.

Emergency Funds

A €20 note shoved up your arsehole for the duration of the holiday in case you need to bribe any of the corrupt local police force. Because, according to Jay, if you don't pay up, they 'take you up to huts in the hills, beat you up and bum ya'.

Lucky, Lucky Men

These characters can be found in most holiday resorts. Usually selling 'Ray Ben' or 'Roy Ban' sunglasses, they'll start you off at around €30 a pair but you can usually haggle them down to €5!

Playing Away

This is a complicated one and can be approached from two viewpoints. First is Jay's, who believes what goes on tour stays on tour. That basically means you can get up to absolutely anything when you're on holiday and it doesn't affect your relationship back home.

Whereas more sensitive Neil has a slightly different approach on account of his 'ethics'. He doesn't believe in cheating, which means no kissing at all, but dry-humping, 'finger-banging', motor-boating, and sex as long as only just the tip goes in is allowed. We don't think you should take either of these guys' advice on this one!

Pussay Patrol

The 'coolest way' to look for girls, whether you're cruising round the suburbs in your mum's Nissan Micra or walking down the Malia strip in your personalised T-shirts.

Suicide Shots

Why drink Tequila the normal way? Instead, for a dare, *Inbetweeners'* Neil decides to snort the salt, down the shot and squeeze the lime into his eye. PLEASE DON'T TRY THIS ONE AT HOME!!!!!

The Richard Branson

Holiday dress code consisting of a white linen shirt and matching white linen trousers. Perfect for poolside lounging or entertaining friends.

THE FUNNIEST QUOTES FROM *THE INBETWEENERS MOVIE*

Since *The Inbetweeners* first hit our screens, fans around the globe have been taking quotes from the show and using them in their lives.

Whether it's Jay's adoption of 'simples' from the well-known Meerkat ads or a cheeky bus-wanker shout, there's been plenty of top moments to choose from and the first film didn't disappoint in providing more ammunition. Here are some of our favourites – enjoy!

Jay: 'Now you've been dumped, we can all go on a mental holiday together... Two weeks of sun, sea, sex, sand, booze, sex, sand, fanny and tits, and booze and sex.'

Jay: 'It'll be like shooting clunge in a barrel.'

Neil: 'S'all right mate, I understand, anyone would miss those tits.'

Simon: 'No, it's not that, Neil.'

Neil: 'Is it her lovely snatch?'

Jay: 'You better bring your wellies because you'll be knee-deep in clunge.'

Will: 'First stop the Minoan Palace in Knossos.'

Jay: 'We haven't come halfway round the world to look at some fucking Greek ruins.'

Neil: 'Yeah, you can see that shit anywhere.'

Jay: 'This girl's so wet for me I can hear the waves breaking in her fanny.'

Simon: 'Jay, you're drunkest. Go over and talk to them.'

Jay: 'Nah. Not me, mate. None of them are as fit as my one outside. Why go for hamburgers when you've got steak at home?'

Will: 'If, like you, you have neither anywhere. It's up to you then, Si.'

Jay: 'Don't you know about foreign police? They take you up a hill, beat you up and then they bum you!'

Neil: 'Yeah, and if they don't kill you, you kill yourself because of the shame of you getting a boner whilst you was being bummed!'

Dinner Lady: 'Don't worry, lads, kitty won't bite. Not now she's been fed.'

Neil: 'I stopped believing in God when I realised it was just dog spelled backwards.'

Neil: 'I think she might be a two-man job.'

Jay: 'My head's more fucked than Neil's dad's arsehole.'

Hotel Manager: 'You shit on floor, €50 fine! EACH TIME!'

Will: 'So smelling like an industrial accident in a Lynx factory and looking like the world's shittest boy-band, we hit the town.'

Mr Gilbert: 'This isn't The Dead Poets Society and I am not that bloke on BBC2 that keeps getting kids to sing in choirs. I especially don't want to hear how well you are settling down at uni or how much growing up you have done in the past twelve months. At best, I am ambivalent towards most of you but some of you I actively dislike, for no other reason than your poor personal hygiene or your irritating personalities. I hope I have made myself clear on this point and, in case any of you think I am joking, I am not. I assure you, once my legal obligation to look after your best interests is removed, I can be one truly nasty fucker. Good luck with the rest of your lives and try not to kill anyone, it reflects very badly on all of us here.'

Will: 'That's it! Neil, you're right. It may not be paradise but it's time we started enjoying this place for what it is.'

Simon: 'A shithole?'

Will: 'Yes, but it's our shithole! So I say we get out there and get royally fucked up on Jay's dead granddad's money!'

Jay: 'He shoots, he scores, right up the vag!'

Will: 'It must reassuring to know that, however bad life gets, you're not me.'

Simon: 'She's also really funny.'

Lucy: 'In what way?'

Simon: 'Well, you know when something's funny and people get it?'

Lucy: 'Yes.'

Simon: 'So in that way. And also in a comedy way.'

Will: 'I like football but I don't like Burnley. Burnley can fuck off.'

Will: 'Jay slept in an ants' nest.'

Jay: 'Oh… The pain.'

THE BITS THEY GOT WRONG

We reckon *The Inbetweeners Movie* is an absolute classic and up there with the best British comedy films. But like us, all the gang aren't perfect and, if you're one of the eagle-eyed fans out there, you may have spotted a few minor mistakes in the film. Here are the ones we know about… see if you had already spotted them.

Simon's dad is regularly being used as a taxi by the gang and it's no different in *The Inbetweeners Movie*. With the boys needing a lift to the airport, he's obviously their first port of call and, much to Simon's embarrassment, he happily uses this time to tell them about his exploits abroad as a young, sexually free lad. This is the first mistake, as the 'dad cab' actually changes completely. As the boys are seen off by their parents into Si's dad's car, they get into a Mazda people carrier but, when the camera shows them on the way, they're in a Volkswagen.

The next movie goof spotted is when the lads arrive at the airport. No, it's not their bright-pink 'pussay patrol' T-shirts but they are the giveaway. When the boys walk up to the check-in desk, the airport worker immediately knows where they're headed because of their stylish attire. 'Malia flight?' she asks sarcastically. But here's where it's wrong, as there isn't actually an airport in Malia. We know the boys are special but surely not special enough to be getting private jets to wherever they choose!

After taking off their hilarious T-shirts under strict instruction from the check-in lady, the boys manage to catch their flight thanks to an extra-long delay, eventually arriving at their sunny destination. When they board the coach on the way to their shitty hotel, sensible Will is told to by the others to catch forty winks after realising his plan of heading straight to bed isn't what the others fancy because they want to hit the strip. Look closely at the comatose nerd and you see the outline of his microphone wire underneath his smart and functional sweater-vest.

Fashion mistakes are the cause of another goof in the movie too and Will's involved again. When the Inbetweener and the lovely Alison are off for a skinny dip late at night on the Malia beach and end up coming across her boyfriend Nicos with another woman, watch Nicos's trousers closely. Don't worry, nothing pops out but, when the Greek bartender is caught by Will as he's 'getting to know' another English holidaymaker, he fumbles around pulling up his trousers while still on the floor. The camera then changes and we see the red-handed Nicos again pulling up his trousers as Will starts feeling very smug about himself.

When Simon and Jay fall out in Malia, it's more *Tom and Jerry* than Froch vs Groves, and more. Not one punch is thrown in the melee and the pair end up in a tight grip on the floor. In fact, it's only a bin in the scene that sees any real violence and this is where the mistake is. As Jay walks away from the fight in a strop, he kicks the nearby bin over next to an empty bench but on the next zoomed-out shot there's suddenly a man sitting there.

And this isn't the only mistake during the epic fight scene – the crew must have been enjoying the fisticuffs so much that they missed a couple of things! If you focus on the people in the background, you'll notice their positioning jumps about. And look out for the extra in the red shirt. He walks past the quad bikes and, after the camera cuts, walks past again.

The big boat party at the end of the film plays host to a couple more of the film's mistakes. It's no surprise, as filming was done out of season off the coast of Magaluf, so it must have been a challenge! The first mistake is right at the start of the scene when we first see the boat. From a distance, we see loads of people having a great time on the top deck but, when the camera zooms in, the shot changes and it's suddenly empty. Now either Jay pulled out his €20 note from his arsehole early or there was a bit of a mix-up during editing. We hope it was the latter!

The other quite obvious goof on the boat is during Simon and Carli's hook-up on the top deck when she's trying to piss off PR prick James by getting with the Inbetweener. As Simon's expressing his feelings for Carli AGAIN, check out her hair. As the camera changes angles, it completely changes from some of her hair being down her back in one shot to the other when it's all down her front.

The last goof of the film is right at the end, as the boys are returning from their epic holiday. As the lads arrive at Gatwick to be greeted by their relieved and surprised parents (all now with gorgeous girls), they actually walk into the arrival hall for domestic flights, definitely not where they'd be if coming back from a holiday to Malia. Maybe the pilot had had enough of the boys and landed at the closest terminal possible!

CHAPTER SIX

THE INBETWEENERS MOVIE 2

It was the summer of 2011 when the first *Inbetweeners* movie surprised the British film industry as a summer blockbuster, setting a new record for the most successful opening weekend ever by a comedy film in the UK. Rocketing to number one in the UK film charts, it stayed at the top spot for a month, grossing an incredible £13.2 million, hurtling the four actors into stardom.

Following on from this success, *The Inbetweeners Movie 2* follows the gang as they head off down-under for an Aussie adventure of epic proportions.

Will They, Won't They?

When fans left the first film, most had one question on their mind: 'Is that the last time we'll see the Inbetweeners?' And the film was such a success with fans and critics that rumours started flying around about a follow-up film, or even another series of the show. This was always denied by the lads, with the feeling that, once the gang went off to university, the show had come to a natural end, something James Buckley talked about to *NME*: 'There are no plans to do any more, unfortunately,' he said. 'I think that will be the last you see of *The Inbetweeners*. I've not been spoken about it at all… I've had interviews in papers just completely made-up – I've not spoken to anyone for six months.'

He then told the music magazine, 'There was an interview in the *Daily Star* where I was quoted saying we were going to do a fourth series and one of the characters was going to die, which wasn't true.' Backing this up again when he spoke to *metro.co.uk*, he said, 'No one wants to see the Inbetweeners older and mature. I think it's got to be the end of *The Inbetweeners*, which is really sad.'

This had *Inbetweeners* fans around the county in tatters. The lads' trip to Malia was so epic, how could the writers and cast call it a day? And then there was a ray of light… In an interview with *screendaily.com*, Christopher Young, who produced the series and first film, admitted that ideas for a second movie had been bounced around: 'If there is a sequel it will come from the creative elements… We've talked about it. In the short term people are dispersing and doing other things but I'm sure in the medium term a sequel is very possible. It won't be immediate but it's definitely not closed.'

Stories around a potential follow-up to the first film continued to circulate, with the *Sun* publishing an article saying that it had been confirmed. It looked like the news fans had been waiting for when the paper reported that a source close to *The Inbetweeners* had told them ideas were being looked into:

> It wasn't easy for any of the guys involved to call it a day after the last film. They were a tight-knit family and really missed each other when it all came to an end.
>
> The writers, Damon Beesley and Iain Morris, have been knocking ideas around for a while and came up with something they thought would be good enough to maintain the high standards they have set.

And Inbetweener Simon Bird added fuel to the fire when he admitted to *Shortlist* that Channel 4 were 'very keen' on a sequel after the surprise success of the first film but that he was as much in the dark as the droves of fans keeping their fingers and toes crossed for another instalment: 'I can tell you that I don't know anything. None of us four have ruled ourselves out but it's about whether Iain and Damon think they can make it as good as the first one. I know they're currently trying to think of ideas and Channel 4 and everyone else are obviously very keen for it to happen.'

And that the four still get on like a house on fire after all those hours spent in that shitty yellow car: 'When we meet up, we immediately fall back into a relationship, which is sort of based on our *Inbetweeners* characters. We're far more mature with our other friends than we are when it's just the four of us together.'

Fellow Inbetweener Blake Harrison then got involved too, admitting to *Digital Spy* that he'd like to thank the brilliant fans of the show and film by giving them a second movie: 'It's nice to give the people who have given you so much and bought your DVDs what they want,' he explained. 'There is a real passion for it to happen though and it would be nice to give those fans a little thank-you with another movie or something else.' But he said that it would only happen with the right script in place:

Everything about a sequel is very much up in the air and it's been that way for quite a long while. So I couldn't tell you one way or another whether it's going to happen. But if it does happen, it will have to be for the right reasons and because the script is good. People are constantly on my Twitter feed talking about it. People all want to know about a sequel and there is obviously a passion for it and the fan-base is always increasing.

So things weren't looking certain for a sequel. There were no confirmed ideas, no real news from the creators or stars and *Inbetweeners* fans across the country were going to school, college and work with very sad faces. That was until *Inbetweeners* co-writer Damon Beesley gave us the strongest hint yet that a sequel was on the cards. He revealed to the *Sun* that the cogs had been turning with him and writing partner Iain Morris for a second movie: 'I don't want to give too much away at this stage but yes, we have been developing an idea for a sequel. We miss working with Simon, Joe, James and even Blake too much not to give it a go.'

This exciting news was backed up by his fellow writer Iain Morris, who tweeted in response to a question about a follow-up film, 'It's far from signed and like Damon said we want to make sure we have a good enough story to tell.'

The writers later went on to tell to the *Radio Times* the

process of getting a new film off the ground, explaining that they didn't just want to rush out a second film on the back of the first and would rather take their time, get it right and make sure they delivered something the fans would really love, maybe even more than the first film (if that's possible!). 'Because the film was genuinely independent, there's no studio breathing down our neck,' said Morris. 'It's down to us to write a script that we think is worth everyone's time; *Inbetweeners* fans are more discerning and vocal than people give them credit for. The last thing any of us wants is a cheap cash-in. At the moment, the script is at version 0.5, so we're getting close… but we're not there yet.'

But Simon (Will) Bird came out and put doubts in all of our minds when he told reporters at the Edinburgh International TV Festival: 'There was a story in the press… but I think that was not quite true, don't believe everything you read. Iain and Damon are thinking about doing one and are trying to think of ideas and that's about as far as it's got. There's no concrete plans, I don't think.' This put everyone back in the dark about what was happening.

2 August 2013: Judgement Day

It's a day *Inbetweeners* fans around the world will remember forever (well, maybe that's a slight exaggeration but it was a pretty cool day). After months of rumours and speculation, back-and-forths between the papers, cast and writers, the genius creators of the show and first film revealed that a sequel to the first film will hit big screens in the UK in August 2014.

The duo released a statement through Channel 4 announcing the fantastic news:

We couldn't be more excited to be making another *Inbetweeners* movie with Simon, Joe, James and Blake. Frankly it's pathetic how much we've all missed each other. A new chapter in the lives of the Inbetweeners feels like the very least we can do to thank the fans for their phenomenal response to the first movie.

Thank you, guys!

On Location

After conquering Europe in the first film with their epic trip to Malia, the new film has the lads travelling halfway around the world. Writers Morris and Beesley revealed that the new film will be set in Australia. 'We can't say too much as we don't want to spoil the jokes for you but what we can exclusively reveal is there will be kangaroos. And Australians. And possibly koalas. Oh, and obviously Jay, Will, Neil and Simon, providing they're let into the country,' he said. 'Thanks so much for all your support, we're hoping to deliver a film that you'll enjoy even more than the last one.'

Crew and cast began filming in Oz on 7 December 2013, with writers Beesley and Morris determined to keep most details of the new adventure under lock and key to keep as many surprises for fans as possible, although Joe Thomas did reveal what he'd like to see in the new movie: 'I would like to see Neil get married... or a funeral – one of them could die.'

Hopefully though Thomas will have left the writing to the others. As much as we love him, we'd HATE to see anything too bad happening to one of the gang. A wedding would be brilliant though!

The team did release a teaser photo of the gang at the Wet N Wild theme park on the Gold Coast just after the Ashes with the caption: 'After another week of English embarrassments in Australia here are four more for you.'

Blake Harrison got involved in the banter, tweeting, 'Here's the first still of the inbetweeners2. It contains 5 jokes. Our faces & Joe's hair.'

Pictures later emerged from the water park of Inbetweener Will at the top of a water slide in a skimpy pair of red trunks, looking less than eager to take the plunge. After his less than successful trip to Thorpe Park, where he accidentally insulted a group of unsuspecting disabled kids, Simon lost his car door and Neil ended up without any clothes, we can't wait to see how the gang get on!

As filming in Oz drew to a close, the gang released a photo to thank the country in typical *Inbetweeners* fashion for its hospitality during filming, showing the four Inbetweeners outside the Sydney Opera House with the message 'G'bye Australia, you've been great to us. It's fair to say you're genuinely a credit to our much maligned convict relocation policy!'

Filming didn't finish there though and, after spending the new year in Oz, the gang headed back to the UK for the final shots. The production team continued to do their best to keep everything under wraps about the new film but pictures did emerge in the *Daily Mail* showing Joe Thomas (Simon) in a variety of cringe-worthy wigs, including a gorgeous, wavy, long brunette number and an eye-watering red Beatles-esque mop. After all of the stick Inbetweener Simon has had over his barnet, it's no surprise he was the one chosen to don some more terrible styles!

New faces

Obviously, our favourite foursome are returning to the big screen for the second *Inbetweeners* film but there are a few new faces that will be making an appearance too.

Harry Potter actor Freddie Stroma is among the new additions to the cast. Stroma had a small part in a *Harry Potter* film, playing Gryffindor student Cormac McLaggen, one year Potter's senior in *Harry Potter and the Deathly Hallows – Part 1 & Part 2*. He appears several times across the two films, with his main scenes being filling in for the famous Potter's friend Ron in a Quidditch match when Ron has been poisoned, and accompanying the other famous part of the Potter trio, Hermione Granger, to Slughorn's Christmas party as her date.

Another new addition to the team is actress Chelsea Li. She has had small roles in a couple of films already, most notably in James Bond blockbuster *Skyfall*. She had a tough challenge with the new *Inbetweeners* film though, this time playing a ladyboy.

Although you won't see this guy, Spencer Millman is another important new addition to the second film. BAFTA nominee Millman has produced some epic stuff during his career, including the weird and wonderful BBC hit *Mighty Boosh*, the hilarious show that has been blamed for ruining Craig David's career *Bo' Selecta* and family favourite *Harry Hill's TV Burp*.

Unfortunately for Inbetweener Will, his previous love interests won't be taking the trip down-under with him. Emily Atack, who played Charlotte 'Big Jugs' Hinchcliffe in the show, revealed that there's no more *Inbetweeners* for her: '*The Inbetweeners* is something I did quite a long time ago now. It was the most amazing thing ever and I wish them all the love and luck in the world but I just think time's gone on now. I watch it and I feel so proud to have been a part of it.'

And it looks like Will's holiday romance didn't go any better either. After what looked like a promising start in Malia for Will and Alison, Laura Haddock told *Mail Online* that she wasn't going to be returning for the second instalment. Fingers crossed that the briefcase mong manages to pull a gorgeous girl from Oz!

Tweets on Set

When it was time for the gang to head off to Oz, Blake Harrison couldn't contain his excitement, announcing the news on Twitter: 'Well it's been confirmed! Me & my fellow inbetweeners will start "Pussay patrolling" down under (where else would you do it?) this week!'

And after their arrival, the excitement continued as, whenever the lads had time away from filming, they'd squeeze in trips to some of Australia's finest attractions, including visiting a wildlife sanctuary to meet some of the local animals. Blake Harrison tweeted: 'Went to a wildlife sanctuary today & picked up some Aussie slang "Get away from that Croc you flaming drongo!"' He also tweeted a picture of himself with a kangaroo ('And the classic "Ooooooh Kangaroo" friend!') and another with a snake ('Strewth mate! That's a snake!').

And on going to a Sydney Sixers cricket match, Blake Harrison tweeted: 'Had a great night watching the @SixersBBL with @James_Buckley & the rest of the inbetweeners lads. #fireycricket,' with writer Iain Morris also getting involved: 'it's always been my dream to watch a boxing day test at the MCG. and this year i get to go. hooray. lucky me. great.'

It looked like the boys were taking things very seriously for their new film, with Buckley tweeting: 'For the first time ever I am learning my lines. You guys are gonna love the slick new professional Inbetweeners movie!'

Until Harrison revealed how his co-star isn't quite the professional he might make himself out as, although he sounds like a great laugh: 'Well it's never mundane working with @James_Buckley because you're constantly ready to throw on a gas mask to protect yourself from his arse.'

And when it was time for the gang to head back to the UK, they had nothing but nice things to say about our neighbours down-under. Harrison tweeted: 'Things better about Oz:

1. The bananas here are massive! Properly massive! (This is not a euphemism)

2. Premiership games r always on!' And more of a sentimental one: 'Thanks Australia! We've had a great time filming here. Hopefully be back soon. P.s. can I take your weather with me?'

It looks like Buckley was ready to return to the UK though, missing his family and kids back home: 'Goodbye Australia! Very sad to leave. Gotta admit I've missed my wife and kids so much tho! So excited to see them! #soppytweet'

'Looking forward to getting home to my wife @Clair_Buckley and those two monsters that live with me!:D #imissmyboys'

Film4 Productions

Film4 Productions will be partly funding the cost of *The Inbetweeners Movie 2*, as they did with the first *Inbetweeners* film along with Bwark Productions (the production company set up by *The Inbetweeners* creators Damon Beesley and Iain Morris).

Since 1982 they have been responsible for backing a large number of films made in the United Kingdom and have been pioneering British talent both behind and in front of the camera. As Film4 have played a major role in taking our favourite show to the big screen, we thought we would take a look at what else they have produced over the years.

12 Years a Slave

An adaptation of the 1853 memoir by Soloman Northup, a free African-American who was kidnapped and sold into slavery to work on the cotton fields in Louisiana. The film was directed by British director Steve McQueen and produced by Brad Pitt, among others. The film gained critical acclaim for its adaptation of a true story, which was reflected at the 2014 Oscars when it was nominated for nine Academy Awards and won three, including Best Picture, Best Supporting Actress (Lupita Nyong'o) and Best Adapted Screenplay. At the BAFTAs in February 2014 the film was nominated for 11 awards and won two: Best Film and Best Actor (Chiwetel Ejiofor).

127 Hours

Based on the book *Between a Rock and a Hard Place*, *127 Hours* tells the story of Aron Ralston, who became trapped by a boulder in an isolated part of the Blue John Canyon in Utah. The film is directed by Academy Award-winning director Danny Boyle, famous for his films *Slumdog Millionaire*, *Shallow Grave*, *28 Days Later* and *Trainspotting*. In 2011 *127 Hours* was nominated for six Oscars and eight BAFTAs.

24 Hour Party People

Film4 teamed up with a number of other benefactors, including the UK Film Council, to produce *24 Hour Party People*, a film about the Manchester music scene between 1976 and 1992 and specifically about music mogul Tony Wilson (played by Steve Coogan) and his company Factory Records. Directed by Michael Winterbottom, the film featured music that shaped a generation and gained critical acclaim for its realism of life in Manchester at that time. Music from the film included the likes of Joy Division, Happy Mondays, New Order and The Jam.

A Life Less Ordinary

Another film directed by Danny Boyle, *A Life Less Ordinary* tells the story of a spoiled rich girl (Cameron Diaz) who gets kidnapped by the janitor of her father's company (Ewan McGregor). They flee to a cabin in the wilderness and, although McGregor's character is the kidnapper, it is clear that the person he has kidnapped is very much in charge. The film received mixed reviews from the critics and on the whole performed poorly at the box office.

Attack the Block

A British sci-fi film, *Attack the Block* comes from the same ilk as movies such as *Shaun of the Dead* and *Hot Fuzz*. The 2011 zombie film was directed by Joe Cornish in his directorial debut. He is most famous for being one half of the comedy duo *Adam & Joe* with his comedy partner Adam Buxton. The production showcased a wealth of British talent, such as Jodie Whittaker and Luke Treadaway. In general, the critics received *Attack the Block* reasonably well and, to date, the review aggregator website *Rotten Tomatoes* awarded the film a score of 90 per cent.

Brassed Off

The 1996 film *Brassed Off* starred Ewan McGregor, Pete Postlethwaite and Tara Fitzgerald. It depicted the plight of workers in a coal-mining town in South Yorkshire who spend much of their time fighting against redundancies in the mine, along with playing in the brass band. The comedy drama film was well received, particularly in mining communities, who thought it was a good reflection on the actual struggles in their area at the time.

Cuban Fury

A 2014 romantic comedy film starring Nick Frost, Rashda Jones and Chris O'Dowd, *Cuban Fury* depicts the life of Bruce (Nick Frost), who aims to reignite his passion for dance in order to win over his new boss. The film was received poorly by the critics with the only real positive remarks being about the likeable aspect of Nick Frost himself.

East is East

Film4 teamed up with BBC Films in 1999 to tell the story of a mixed-ethnic family growing up in Salford, Manchester in 1971. The film, directed by Damien O'Donnell, went on to win Best British Film at the 2000 BAFTA awards ceremony and Best Comedy Film at the British Comedy Awards. The sequel, which received no funding from Film4, was released in 2010.

Four Weddings and a Funeral

Another Hugh Grant masterclass in rom-com! The British film in 1994 was, and still is, a cult hit and remains a Richard Curtis classic. Film4 (then called Channel Four Films) funded the production, along with Polygram and Working Title Films. *Four Weddings* went on to win four BAFTAs, including Best Film, Best Direction, Best Actor and Best Supporting Actress, and was also nominated for two Academy Awards.

In Bruges

This 2008 black comedy featured Colin Farrell in the leading role alongside Brenden Gleeson and Ralph Fiennes. The film about two Irish hit-men didn't make much of a splash at the box office. However, it would go on to gain critical acclaim.

Nowhere Boy

This Film4-funded production depicted the story of John Lennon's youth. The film followed John Lennon through his adolescent years, meeting Paul McCartney to form The Quarrymen, and his life when he became separated from his mother. *Nowhere Boy* was nominated for four BAFTAs in 2009.

Seven Psychopaths

A film directed by *In Bruges* director Martin McDonagh, *Seven Psychopaths* was a dark comedy starring Colin Farrell, Sam Rockwell, Woody Harrelson and Christopher Walken about a man who has dreams of becoming a screenwriter but gets more than he bargained for with his group of friends and acquaintances.

Sexy Beast

Fox Searchlight Pictures and Film4 distributed this British crime film starring Ray Winstone, Ben Kingsley, Amanda Redman and Ian McShane. *Sexy Beast* has become somewhat of a cult film since its premiere in the year 2000 and gained very favourable reviews from the critics.

Shaun of the Dead

One of Britain's most successful comedy films, *Shaun of the Dead* has gained cult status as the original 'zom-com'. The film starred the comedy duo Simon Pegg and Nick Frost, who would also go on to feature in the films *Hot Fuzz* and *The World's End*.

Slumdog Millionaire

Danny Boyle won critical acclaim and a raft of awards for this 2008 drama about a young man from India who exceeds expectations on the game show *Who Wants to be a Millionaire*. In 2009 the film cleaned up at the awards ceremonies, picking up eight Oscars (Best Film, Best Director, Best Adapted Screenplay, Best Cinematography, Best Original Score, Best Original Song, Best Film Editing, Best Sound Mixing) and seven BAFTAs (Best Film, Best Director, Best Adapted Screenplay, Best Cinematography, Best Film Music, Best Editing, Best Sound).

The Crying Game

Film4, Palace Pictures, British Screen and Miramax produced this 1992 British psychological thriller starring Stephen Rea, Miranda Richardson and a young Forest Whitaker. The film depicted the experience of a young man who was a member of the IRA. It was nominated for six Academy Awards, winning one for Best Original Screenplay.

The Iron Lady

Meryl Streep won an Oscar for her performance as Margaret Thatcher in the 2011 biopic, which also starred Jim Broadbent, Anthony Head (father of Emily Head) and Richard E. Grant. Film4 teamed up with a number of different studios, including Canal+ and the UK Film Council. *The Iron Lady* won two Academy Awards in 2011 (Best Actress and Best Make-up) and two BAFTAs (Best Actress, Best Make-up and Hair).

The Lovely Bones

Film4 and Paramount Pictures brought us this Peter Jackson-directed film in 2009 based on the bestselling novel of the same name. *The Lovely Bones* is the story the disappearance of a 14-year-old girl in Pennsylvania and stars Mark Wahlberg and Rachel Weisz.

This is England

One of Britain's most critically acclaimed films, *This Is England* thrust director Shane Meadows into the limelight, and he would go on to direct the TV adaptations of the film, *This Is England '86* and *This Is England '88*. And a third TV offering is rumoured to be in the pipeline for 2015. The film followed the story of a group of young skinheads in England in 1983 and how their sub-culture shaped their lives.

Trainspotting

One of the biggest cult films of the 20th Century, *Trainspotting* was directed by Danny Boyle and followed the lives of a group of friends living in a tough part of Edinburgh and followed their battle with drug addiction. Starring Ewan McGregor, Jonny Lee Miller and Robert Carlyle, the film was nominated for three BAFTA awards in 1995.

The Inbetweeners Movie

How could we leave this film out? In 2011 Film4 combined with Bwark Productions (Iain Morris and Damon Beasley's production company) and Young Films (the company started by music and film producer Christopher Young) to produce the coming-of-age comedy film of the year! The film, which was released in August 2011, raked in over $88 million in worldwide box office revenue and at the time held the record for the most successful opening weekend for a comedy film in the UK. Reviewers also loved the film, with *Empire Online* calling it 'gag for gag the funniest film of the summer' and *The Guardian* describing Simon Bird as 'a young David Mitchell trapped in an episode of *Ibiza Uncovered*'. For the second *Inbetweeners* film, Film4 teamed up with Bwark Productions once again to create what will surely be another summer hit film!

Across the Pond

It's not just the British *Inbetweeners* that will be hitting the big screen. It's not known whether creators Morris and Beesley will have any involvement with the film *Virgins America* but it has been announced that English film and television director Jim Field Smith will be directing the American adaptation.

The US TV remake wasn't received well across the pond and, just four months after launching in the summer of August 2012 on MTV, the show was axed due to poor ratings.

Jim Field Smith has numerous directing credits under his belt, including *Episodes*, fronted by ex-*Friends* star Matt Le Blanc and *Shaun of the Dead* star Tamsin Greig, and 2010 film *She's Out of My League*, starring up-and-coming Hollywood actor Jay Baruchel.

Did You Know?

Thomas, Buckley, Bird and Harrison are set to earn £2.5 million each for reprising their roles – a huge increase after their £100,000 pay cheque the first time round.

As well as being a massive box-office success, the first film sold an incredible 1.9 million DVDs.

Writing duo Iain Morris and Damon Beesley must be some of the most modest guys out there, describing the first *Inbetweeners* film as 'a ninety-minute version of the TV show' and an 'OK British film'. We reckon it was pretty special and, judging by its performance at the box office, so do a lot of other people.

CHAPTER SEVEN

OUR TOP 10 MOMENTS

Just like most *Inbetweeners* fans out there, we have our favourite moments from the three series and first film. With so many best bits to choose from it's tricky to narrow it down to just 10 and you might not agree with everything here but take a look at our top-10 picks and see what you think. (Feel free to cross them out if you don't agree – unless this is a library book!)

10. Simon vomiting

Think all the way back to the second episode of the first series, 'Bunk Off', and you'll remember number 10 in our top-10 moments. With all the parents at work, the lads have decided to take a day off school, get some alcohol and have a party in a poorly planned tactic to get the interest of some girls – poorly planned as they soon realise all of the girls they know are in school.

Undeterred, the four boys partake in a drinking game, during which Simon declares his love for school-mate Carli D'Amato. This was already clear to the others but, fuelled by alcohol, Simon decides a grand gesture is needed and proceeds to spray-paint his feelings onto Carli's parents' front driveway.

Unbelievably, this gets Si an invite round to the house later and he thinks his luck is in. But after consuming copious amounts of alcohol throughout the day, his plan begins to quickly unravel and he projectile vomits all over Carli's unsuspecting kid brother!

9. Shit sniffing

Most *Inbetweeners* fans hate James, the PR rep in the first film. He runs Simon over on his quad bike, steals all of his clothes and throttles Jay in a club. Basically, he's a bit of a prick and that's why 'shit sniffing' is one of our favourite moments.

In the boat-party scene at the end of the first film, after insulting Inbetweener Jay and his new girlfriend Jane, James tells Jay he needs a note to take some cocaine. What he hasn't realised though is that Jay pulls out the Euros he's had stashed up his arse all holiday in case he needs a bribe for the corrupt foreign police.

The unsuspecting PR guru James heads to the toilets to take his coke and ends up with a sizeable chunk of Jay's shit on the end of his nose! What's better is that he doesn't even realise it's there and spends the rest of the scene wondering why his usual chat-up lines aren't working with the girls.

8. Kids' toilet

When the lads arrive at what can only be described as Malia's –

and possibly the world's – shittest hotel in the first film, they take a look around at all of the amenities the apartment they're staying in for the next two weeks has to offer: dirty fridge with half a can of dog food – check; sofa bed covered in suspicious dark stains – check; kids' toilet, aka bidet (bumwash) – check. But the European sophistication of a bidet is lost on the lads and Jay explains to Neil, who questions this porcelain mystery, that it's a kids' toilet for 'checking your kid's shit before you flush it… that's the continentals, innit. They're dirty.'

So later in the film, when Neil finds himself full to the brim with beer and kebab meat, he decides to mix things up a bit and take a massive dump in the bidet, only to find it doesn't flush!

The scene ends with Jay and Simon poking and prodding the huge shit with little success and Jay asking, 'Neil, what the fuck has gone into that? Have you been eating teargas?'

Blake Harrison later revealed on Twitter: 'To answer a common question the shit in the bidet was made of chocolate. The props dept then ate it. It was disturbing to watch.'

EURGH! We don't even think Jay Cartwright would pull a stunt like that!

7. Will's gig

In the second episode of the third series, 'Unlucky in Love', Inbetweener Simon, in a desperate bid to impress a girl in the year below, tells her that he's going to the same gig as her at The Enterprise on Friday night and that he'll bring drugs.

On the night, and after Jay's supply fails to materialise, the lads eventually manage to score some weed. After it's been passed round, Jay starts giving Will stick because he didn't smoke any. Annoyed and determined to prove him wrong, Will takes all of the remaining weed and engulfs it in one bite! He quickly enters a confused state and comes out with some classic quotes: 'You need to call an ambulance right now because I can't use the phone, my arms don't work and my hands are sausages,' and, 'Call an ambulance and tell them I'm in a bubble and everything is very flat.'

His wishes are granted and the hilariously embarrassing scene ends with Will being driven off in an ambulance, arms flying about everywhere as if he can't control them!

6. Ham-and-goggles wank

Another one from the first film, this one is horrible but hilarious. The camera pans to Inbetweener Jay's bedroom, where he's seen sitting on his bed in his boxers and a Brazil top, wearing a snorkelling mask and a ski glove, watching a live Eastern European sex show with a packet of ham!

'You promise this is gonna be proper filthy?' he asks just before his poor mother and sister walk in to break the news of his grandfather's death while the web-cam girl tells him, 'You' got a lady there, you bad boy. Has she got nice titties? Suck on the lady's titties, suck them, go on!' Awkward is not the word!

5. Simon's bollock

It's the charity fashion show and Simon is delighted to be involved, as this is his chance to impress Carli, the girl he's been hanging around like a bad rash for ages.

And it looks like his luck might be in as the guy who's meant to be doing the final catwalk has been ditched on account of his disgustingly hairy back. So it's now or never for Si; impress here and this could finally be his chance to get the girl of his dreams.

The speedos and hat ensemble he's been asked to wear is revealing to say the least but Si doesn't care as long as it will impress Carli. So despite Jay and Neil telling him that if he gets a boner, the whole school will see, Simon heads out to strut his stuff down the catwalk.

So focused on not getting a boner, however, Simon hasn't realised that his bollock is actually hanging out of his costume for the whole school to see, including his dad and the less than impressed Carli, who storms off.

What makes this scene even funnier is that actor Joe Thomas who plays Simon turned down the option of a 'stunt-ball' and opted to go with the real deal. Brave man!

4. So little, so little

The lads are in Malia and a kid by the pool has been getting right on Jay's tits. After first kicking Jay in the legs and then pushing him into the pool when he and Neil were trying to impress some 'chicas', Jay decides to get his own back. So he picks up the little runt and holds him face down over the pool. 'Ah no, I no swim, please, Mr, I no swim, I beg you...' screams the little kid and, in a moment of caring, Jay actually lets the kid go and puts him down without even dunking his head.

It looks like the drama might be over until the little kid runs behind Jay and, in front of a load of sunbathers, pulls down his Man Utd shorts to reveal his pubic hair shaved into the shape of an arrow pointing to his penis!

The other holidaymakers burst into laughter and the kid laughs and points at Jay's nether regions and says, 'So little, so little.' The red-faced Jay launches the kid into the pool to get his own back but still comes off like the bad guy after it turns out that the kid wasn't lying when he said he couldn't swim. Luckily, a couple of muscle-bound fellas are there to jump in and rescue the kid, making Jay look even worse than he already does.

3. Will shitting himself

It's exam time at Rudge Park Comprehensive in the final episode of series two and studious Will is determined to ace his subjects. The only problem is he gets so caught up with creating a revision schedule that he doesn't leave himself much time to actually revise, as he realises when Simon asks how things are going: 'Yeah, not bad, pretty good, got an excellent schedule, colour coded. I'm balancing my time well, got some drinks here to help, Pro Plus, that sort of thing… and nothing's fucking going in…'

But despite Simon's advice to get more sleep and to lay off the energy drinks because they make your shit 'come out too fast' and like 'rusty water', Will continues with his plan.

By the time the exam comes Will has consumed copious amounts of energy drinks and, after being refused permission to leave the exam hall for the fourth time in an hour to go to the bathroom again, he starts to really struggle. The belly rumbles get so loud that other pupils start to notice and he ends up shitting himself right in the middle of the exam and is forced to waddle to the toilet with Head of Sixth Mr Gilbert: 'I thought it was a fart, sir. I thought it was safe.'

The event finishes with Will having a pint with the rest of sixth form, wearing a pair of lost-property undies and trousers and holding his shit-covered clothes in a carrier bag.

2. Bus wankers

In episode four of the second series, the Inbetweeners decide to head off for a night out to the London clubs in Simon's shitty yellow car.

The trip starts off well, with a chat between the lads about who's fittest – Will's mum or Neil's sister – then Jay leans out of the window and shouts at the top of his voice at unsuspecting members of the public waiting at a bus stop, 'Bus wankers!'

All of the lads think it's hilarious, even Simon, who has been shitting himself about the drive. And just as the four reach the streets of London, Jay again screams, 'Bus wankers!' out of the front passenger-side window. The problem this time is that the guys are caught in a traffic jam and a couple of 'heavies' who were at the bus stop catch up with the 'bitchmobile'.

Leaning into Simon's window, one of the guys throttles Si and tells his mate, 'I'd rather be a bus wanker than drive that yellow piece of shit.' For a moment the lads all bottle it but, once the danger is clearly over, they start taking the piss out of Simon for shaking with fear.

We LOVE this scene and it makes us scream with laughter each time we watch it but please don't shout 'bus wankers' out of your or your mate's car!

1. The Malia dance

By far our favourite *Inbetweeners* scene so far, the lads' dance in Malia was an instant hit with fans and *Inbetweeners* newbies alike.

After a group of girls walk in to the absolutely empty club the lads have been lured into, Jay offers up a bit of advice: 'You don't just walk up to a group of girls and introduce yourself. It's creepy… You dance over near them, make the eyes and get 'em to dance over with ya… and then after a bit, you stand up behind 'em and pretend to slap 'em and fuck 'em up the arse.'

Ignoring the last bit, even Will thinks Jay's advice sounds about right and, to the sounds of 'We No Speak Americano', Neil launches into a frantic body-pop in the direction of the girls, followed by Simon pulling off some sort of skipping and drumming move, with Will at the back galloping from side to side!

The girls in the film aren't too impressed by the awkward moves but fans love the dance so much that they're always asking Blake Harrison, who plays Neil, to do a little rendition. He revealed to *Digital Spy* that he once got asked by a bunch of his beloved Millwall fans to knock out a performance: 'I went to Wembley and I was walking up Wembley and I heard, "Oi, Neil, do the dance!"' said Harrison. 'And it suddenly turns into a chant. "Do the Dance! Do the Dance! Do the Dance!" It's all meant in a lovely way… but no, I didn't do it.'

Despite all of this attention though, Harrison said he's more than happy to hear from a fan when he's out and about:

Sometimes you're out on a night with the girlfriend and drunk people want a hug or a photo but it's always a compliment. It's meant in a lovely way. So even if you've got chicken in your mouth and someone's taking a photo, these are the guys who love the show, buy the DVDs, so it's always a nice thing. I never understood why people complain loads about fans. I've never said no to a photo.

And it's not just regular Joes on the street that are fans of the dance. In fact, the One Direction guys even got involved during an audience-interaction segment of a concert. First asked by a fan on the big screen, 'What is the weirdest dance move you know?' and after performing a few, another fan replies, 'Inbetweeners' dance?' And fairplay to the lads, who stand in a line and copy the famous moves of Simon, Will and Neil to thousands of screaming fans. They definitely looked cooler than the original guys doing it!

CHAPTER EIGHT

EVERY CHARACTER EVER – FULL A-Z GUIDE

Think you're the biggest *Inbetweeners* fan? Well, here's your chance to test your skills. Here we've got EVERY character that's appeared in the three series and the first film – see if you can remember them all.

Alastair
One of school-bully Mark Donovan's cronies, Alastair makes a brief appearance in the show during the first episode when things don't go quite to plan for new kid Will McKenzie, making him a target for Mark and his mates throughout the three series.

Alison
We first see Alison when the lads are on the coach from the airport to their hotel in Malia in the first film. Neil is immediately impressed by her and the other three girls – 'tidy

minge, ten o'clock' – but Jay tells him that four girls is just too much at one time for him on a coach, unlike the time when he had sex with an entire netball team in a luxury caravan! Smell a bit of bullshit?

Unbelievably, the lads' chance to speak to the lovely Alison isn't over as, along with her mates, she goes to Marco's Club, the first dive they visit on the Malia strip. After witnessing the infamous dance, staggeringly, she seems to instantly take a shine to Will, despite the fact that he takes the piss out of her Greek boyfriend Nicos for a good five minutes, thinking that she's being ironic, when she's not!

After finding out that Will is a virgin, Alison forms a pact with the Inbetweener that, if he doesn't have sex in the next year, she'll sleep with him. Soon afterwards, Will thinks he's in luck when the pair go skinny dipping, only to run in to Alison's boyfriend, who is cheating with another girl, which (for a change) leads to Will acting like a bit of a tit.

For a time it looks like things might be off for the pair but Alison has a change of heart and at the boat party at the end of the film, she ends up kissing Will and bringing the pact forward, with the added bonus of them becoming boyfriend and girlfriend. We reckon Will has hit the jackpot with the lovely Alison, who is WELL out of his league!

Becky

Appearing in 'Caravan Club' in the first series of the show, Becky is described by Jay as the slut of the campsite and, after showing some interest in Simon, the pair end up hitting it off at a terrible site party later that night. Becky likes Simon but is definitely not as keen as the sex-starved Inbetweener is and, when he whips out his tackle outside of the party, she screams at him and is never seen again.

Benji Cartwright

Little Benji is the Cartwright family's dog, who loves nothing more than to watch Inbetweener Jay having a wank. Sadly, in the third series of the show, while Jay is staying at Will's house to have a wank in peace, we find out that Benji has died.

Jay's sister

We meet Jay's younger sister in the first film, where she and her mum unfortunately walk in on Jay having a wank with a packet of ham and a snorkel… to break the news to him that their granddad has died. Awkward.

Jay Cartwright

Hopefully, you know who this one is! Filthy mouthed, bullshitting, serial-wanking, pussay patrolling, caravan-clubbing, pube-shaving Jay Cartwright is the mate you love to hate. If he's not locked in his room with his parents' credit card and a packet of ham, he's telling his mates about his latest orgy in a caravan with a load of Swedish models.

On the outside, Jay puts up the bullshitting front that he's 'been there, done it' but every now and then we get a bit of an insight into his more sensitive side. Underneath all of the stories, we reckon Jay is a pretty decent lad and this is seen right at the end of *The Inbetweeners Movie* when he's hand-in-hand with new love Jane.

Of course, he's absolutely filthy and hilarious too and here are plenty of his best quotes to keep you amused:

'When I fingered her, she shit down my arm.'

'I had one bent over the table here, there was one up here who I was fingering and I was just toe fucking the one on the floor.' (About his caravan orgy.)

'Friend, friend, let's go for a drive sometime, friend... I'm not your fucking friend!'

'We don't need a plan. We go in there, buy some drinks and wait for the gash to form an orderly queue.'

'A car is like a mobile pulling machine. Forget about Carli, forget about all of the girls at this school. There is a whole world of pussy out there.'

'I'll be up to my nuts in guts, shagging those two sisters from Caravan Club.'

'I wouldn't shag any of the skanky girls around here, mate. Except for your mum.'

'Sounds like a bent version of *Brokeback Mountain*.'

'Two weeks of sun, sea, booze, minge, fanny and sex.'

'While you two decide who gets first go on each other's cocks, I'm getting out there.'

'The gash isn't gonna fuck itself, ya know.'

'We haven't come halfway around the world to look at some boring fucking Greek ruins.'

'I'm on holiday, you can't be too drunk.'

'He shoots, he scores, right up the vag.'

'You better bring your wellies because you'll be knee-deep in clunge.'

'This girl's so wet for me I can hear the waves breaking in her fanny.'

'Why go for hamburgers when you have steak at home?'

'She's already seen the crown jewels: my bell-end.'

'On holiday in Spain one year, me and my mate took a pedalo out and went to Africa.'

'Don't worry about me, mate, I'm up to my neck in sluts at the moment. Maybe I'll bring my new fuck buddy along, that little blonde barmaid from the Fox and Hounds.'

'My head's more fucked than Neil's dad's arsehole.'

'All right, Yves Saint Leponce, what's going on here then?'

Mrs Cartwright

The poor mother of Jay and wife of Terry, Mrs Cartwright has to put up with a lot. We see her in three episodes of the series and also in the first film, often having to put up with Jay's lies and disgusting behaviour. The worst situation the meek Mrs Cartwright finds herself in is in the opening of the film when she has to break the news to Jay that his granddad has died. The only problem is that, when she walks in on her son, he's sitting on the bed with a packet of ham, wanking over a live Eastern European sex show.

Terry Cartwright

When we first meet Jay's dad Terry, it quickly becomes apparent where Jay gets his lies and rudeness from. The only thing is, however, Terry has had a lot longer to practise, so he's really not a very likeable character at all.

Like all dads, Terry goes out of the way to embarrass his son but, unlike other dads, he manages to embarrass everyone else too. When the lads go to Caravan Club with the Cartwrights, Terry stinks the place out when in the caravan toilet; when Jay gets a girlfriend, Terry is the one who gives the advice that ends up finishing the relationship; and just before the boys go off to Malia, Terry manages to insult Neil's dad too.

Chloe

It's exam time at Rudge Park Comp in the second series of the show when we meet Chloe. For once in his life, Jay proves to the others that his stories aren't always bullshit when he tells the lads he met Chloe at the bus stop one day and shows the lads plenty of pics of the two of them looking very happy with each other.

Chloe and Jay are getting on great until Jay's dad starts putting doubts in his son's mind and advises him to keep tabs on Chloe constantly because she'll probably get off with another lad. Put off by Jay's stalker-ish behaviour, Chloe splits with him at the end of the episode just as Jay's about to introduce her to the other boys, and we never see her again.

Alan Cooper

They say you can't choose your family and we're not sure if Inbetweener Simon would ever choose Alan as a dad. Appearing in the three series and first film, Alan is a bit of a taxi and is usually seen driving the lads about.

Much to Simon's embarrassment but the other lads' delight, he usually uses this time to talk about his sex life as a teen, telling the boys on their way to the airport in the first film, 'Me and my mates went to Magaluf. Shagaluf we called it. Should have called it Shagalot, and hard, anything that moved… you'll find girls just seem to let themselves go a bit more abroad. It's like as soon as they smell the sun cream, they get wet. Your mother's the same even now.'

Alan is played by comedy actor Martin Trenaman, who has worked on a few comedy golds during his career, including 1990s smash *Spaced*, *The Mighty Boosh*, *Never Mind the Buzzcocks* and *PhoneShop*.

Favourite quote: 'Come on, Simon, me and your mum like doing it as well, you know.'

Andrew Cooper

Inbetweener Simon's kid brother who, like all little brothers, does his best to annoy Simon throughout the first three series, including giving him plenty of stick about his little yellow car and his 'I love Carli D'Amato' stunt when Jay tells Simon, 'He's made you look a right knob.' Just what all younger brothers should do!

Pamela Cooper

The first call for Simon when he needs money, Pam appears to be like most mums: kind, caring and concerned with her son's comings and goings. But it's when her husband Alan tells the lads she's a demon in the sack that we learn of a different side to her!

Favourite quote: 'Just because Kevin's gay doesn't mean he's a paedophile!'

Simon Cooper

With 'hair like the Statue of Liberty', a shitty yellow car, very hairy balls (well, at least the right one) and an unhealthy obsession for Carli D'Amato, Simon is, unbelievably, the Inbetweener who gets the most attention from the ladies, although it doesn't always pan out. There have been a few girls in his life throughout the series and first film: Carli, Lauren, Tara and Lucy.

It's actually Si who, way back in the first series, reluctantly took Will under his wing to form the gang we know and love and he's often the one who pushes the others to get involved in adventures, like clubbing in London and the trip to Warwick. It's even his break-up with Carli that gives the lads the excuse to take the famous trip to Malia in the first film.

Favourite quotes:

'Work, you stupid, fucking thing! Get big! Get big!'

'I'm gonna fuck your fucking fanny off, you twat!'

'What… so if I spunked in your face, it would be yours?'

'Wayne Pooney, Take Shat… Brad Shit… Vladimir Pootin.'

'Yeah, that's right, I've had two hundred and ten wanks and my cock's like a Pepperami!'

'You think I don't fucking know that? I know that better than anyone! I know it's floppy!'

'He seems a bit weird. He asked me if I've tried the "Sleeping Beauty".'

'You spunked your pants in the common room during the day when there were people around… Then your pubes fell out… I think this is way out of my league.'

Sadie Cunningham

Classmate of Inbetweener Jay, Sadie is a victim of theft by Jay twice in the show. Once when he steals hair-removal cream from her bag to put down Will's trousers (leading him to stuff a wig down there) and again when he steals an invite to Louise Graham's house party (where Will ends up covered in dog shit). Lucky girl!

Carli D'Amato

Family friend and Inbetweener Simon's first love, Carli appears in all three series of the show and the first film. Simon never quite manages to get with her during the series, despite several efforts to attract her attention, including going on a night out in London wearing a tramp's shoes, spray-painting his affections for her on the front drive of her parents' house and forfeiting his own studies to help her revise for the GCSE exams.

But at the start of the first film it looks like Simon's luck might be in as he's sitting on Carli's bed kissing her, until she utters the dreaded words, 'Simon, we need to talk,' going on to tell him that she wants to break up to enjoy her summer holiday and uni life as a singleton.

She gets hitched again pretty quickly, when she meets PR rep and all-round cock James in Malia but, after a few run-ins with him, things fall apart and Carli decides to use Si to get back at the other lad. Thankfully, after a while, Simon realises what she's doing and opts for the much nicer Lucy, which we were happy with!

Chris D'Amato

Poor Chris only appears in a couple of episodes of the show and both times he's subjected to Simon's love-crazed antics. The first occasion is when Simon goes to see Carli after bunking off school and drinking all day. The mixture of lust and cheap liquor affects him badly and he ends up spewing all over little Chris's face.

The next time is when the young kid is at home sleeping, only to be woken up by Simon climbing through his bedroom window, mistaking it for Carli's room. We reckon the little blighter is probably going to end up needing some counselling one day!

Mrs D'Amato

Mother to Inbetweener Simon's long-term love interest Carli. We hear Carli moaning about her mum in the series but we only see Mrs D'Amato once, when the lads are bunking off from school in the first series and Jay decides to embarrass Simon by pointing at him and shouting to her, 'Oi, he wants to suck your Carli's tits.'

Steve D'Amato

Father of Carli, Steve is less than impressed by the actions of the young Simon chasing the heart of his daughter. The first thing Simon does to piss him off is when he decides to show his feelings for Carli by spray-painting his love in a mural on the driveway of their family home. His second screw-up is when he tries to sneak into Carli's home in a fit of romance but ends up in her kid-brother's room like some sort of prowler.

David

Fellow new-starter with Will at Rudge Park Comp, David falls well into the 'freaks' category at the school and even Will wants to avoid being seen with him and the other new-starters in an attempt to get into one of the cool gangs at school. Obviously, this fails.

Daisy

It's not very often that a girl shows interest in Inbetweener Will but his neighbour and former babysitter Daisy takes a shine to him. Appearing in the fifth episode of the second series, 'The Duke of Edinburgh Awards', Daisy works at a retirement home where Will and the gang end up doing work experience.

She makes a deal to go on a date with Will when he covers one of her shifts and, unbelievably, things look like they're going well. After dinner, she invites him back to her place, where she is shocked to discover that Will is wearing a 'pubic wig', thanks to Jay squirting hair-removal cream down his trousers at school. Funnily enough, this puts her right off and we never see Daisy again!

Dean

Appearing in the fourth episode of the second series, 'Night out in London', Dean is the character Carli's mate chooses over Inbetweener Will. Dean is played by Jonny Sweet, close friend of Simon Bird (Will) and Joe Thomas (Simon) outside of the show, and co-writer with the pair of the Sky1 show *Chickens*.

Drug Dealer

When Jay's 'regular' dealer fails to produce because he's in Afghanistan on a drug-sourcing trip (yeah, right), the lads approach a guy at the gig who they guess to be a drug dealer. What they don't expect is the dealer to take offence to them assuming his profession: 'Oh, so you want to buy drugs. And you came to me. Why? Because I'm black? You saw a black guy at a gig and thought, "He must be a drug dealer?" Why should I deal to you? Why should I deal to two little suburban racists who see me as some kind of stereotype? I'm at university!'

The drug dealer is played by UK rapper and comedian Doc Brown and has appeared in Ricky Gervais's *Derek* and the Comic Relief special of *The Office*, where he showed off his acting and rapping skills.

Donna

One of Inbetweener Neil's older ladies in Malia, Donna can be seen getting 'motor-boated' by the teen in the resort club, Marco's. In an interview with *metro.co.uk*, Blake described how this wasn't as much fun as it looked for his character: 'It's incredibly awkward when you meet someone for the first time, shake their hand and know that five minutes later you're going to have your head in between their boobs.' Poor Donna!

Mark Donovan

School bully and enemy of Inbetweener Will, Mark appears throughout the first three series of the show. He takes an immediate dislike to Will and decides to plaster pics of him taking a shit all around the school building, and his feelings of hatred grow throughout the show as he learns that Will has feelings for his ex, Charlotte Hinchcliffe.

His run-ins with Will include chasing him after he hits a disabled woman with a Frisbee, putting a bin on his head and threatening to beat him up at the Christmas party. An all-round nice guy then.

Favourite quote: 'Is that your mum? She is fit! Lovely to meet you, Mrs McKenzie.'

Hannah Fields

It's not often that we see one of the lads getting lucky in love but for Inbetweener Simon, Hannah looks like a bit of a cert. In the second episode of the second series, after sending him a Valentine's card, she meets up with the older Inbetweener and, after slipping him some vodka in an under-18's disco, she proceeds to wank him off at the edge of the dance floor, with the other Inbetweeners watching in amazement.

Fwiend, aka Car Fwiend, aka Football Fwiend

Mates with Inbetweener Jay after apparently meeting him during trials for West Ham (clearly one of Jay's bullshit stories), he makes his only appearance in the first-series episode 'Will Gets a Girlfriend'.

He's first introduced at a house party, where the other Inbetweeners quickly begin to question how Jay knows him and take the piss out of Jay's vagueness in explaining who he is: 'He's a friend... just some guy.'

He seems like a really nice guy but, in a bit of a breakdown, Jay later ends up jumping all over the car he offered to let him have a go in, after taking loads of 'Fwiend' stick from the others.

Phil Gilbert

Head of Sixth Form at Rudge Park Comp, Mr Gilbert hates the kids he's responsible for and has a particular dislike for Inbetweener Will. The pair have several run-ins throughout the series and Gilbert's no-bullshit personality clashes harshly with Will's condescending tone.

When it comes to the ladies though, he can be a very different character. When Inbetweener Neil tries it on with Biology teacher Miss Timms, Gilbert is straight over there to sort it out. He also shows a very clear interest in MILF and mum to Will, Polly McKenzie. Who can blame him there though?!

Although Gilbert appears at the beginning of the film, wishing the sixth form a less than heartfelt goodbye, and briefly at the end, riding down the Malia strip on a quad bike, there's also a deleted scene that didn't make the final cut.

When Simon and Jay have had their pathetic spatter and split up, Will and Simon come across a group chanting in a bar. On further inspection, they find the Head of Sixth in the middle of the crowd downing a yard of ale in a pair of skimpy trunks.

Favourite quote: 'This isn't The Dead Poets Society and I am not that bloke on BBC2 that keeps getting kids to sing in choirs. I especially don't want to hear how well you are settling down at uni or how much growing up you have done in the past twelve months. At best, I am ambivalent towards most of you but some of you I actively dislike… once my legal obligation to look after your best interests is removed, I can be one truly nasty fucker. Good luck with the rest of your lives and try not to kill anyone, it reflects very badly on all of us here.'

David Glover

Mates with school bully Mark Donovan, David Glover is the Rudge Park Comp pupil that supposedly got with Jay's love interest Chloe before they met.

Favourite quote: 'Leave the specky short-arse alone. He's organised a good party.' (To Donovan, about Will.)

Chris Groves

It's questionable as to whether Chris is actually a real character in the show, as it's only bullshitter Jay who ever references him as his mate in Year 13 of Rudge Park Comp.

Lauren Harris

Simon's definitely the Inbetweener who gets the most attention from the girls (although he always manages to screw it up). He catches new girl Lauren's eye on the geography and sociology fieldtrip to Swanage in the second series of the show, despite Will's attempts to impress her with his Yoda impression.

Things fall apart between the pair when Lauren and the rest of the people on the trip see Simon naked on a rowing boat, with just a sock covering his unmentionables.

Heike

Jay's last experience with a Dutch girl – maybe he wasn't going to be taking any chances this time around: 'When I fingered her, she shit down my arm.' Heike, the girl from Holland, was in for one hell of a night!

Jay and Neil are mesmerised by the Dutch girl (despite her having the flu) and, when she tells the pair to 'have a super-fun night', they somehow take it the wrong way and think she's coming onto them, reaching a few conclusions: 'fucking hell, she's fit' (Neil), 'she looks like she loves cock' (Jay) and that 'there are three things you need to know about European birds… they're filthy, they're hairy and they don't mind if you wipe it on the curtains' (again Jay!).

So when Heike's flatmate Joe and his mates wind Jay up by telling him that she loves 'young meat', he decides to head off to her room to ask for a shag. Unsurprisingly, she's less than impressed and Jay and the others are swiftly thrown out.

Charlotte Hinchcliffe

'Big Jugs' is the most popular and sexually experienced pupil at Rudge Park Comp, claiming to have had 'eleven lovers' in the first series of the show (imagine how many it is now!). She appears in episodes across the different series of the programme and, after a split with school bully Mark Donovan, is looking for some fresh meat.

Geeky Inbetweener Will takes an immediate liking to her when he starts at Rudge Park and, although everyone including Will thinks she's well out of his league, at a house party the pair hit it off and a 'sort of' relationship blossoms.

After some heavy petting, Charlotte invites Will over but, after what can only be described as a very awkward attempt at sex, she leaves things with the clearly inexperienced Inbetweener. The two have a few more run-ins but it never quite works out, despite the fact that Charlotte clearly does like Will.

When French exchange student Patrice stays with Simon's family, he ends up getting involved in some extra-curricular activities with Charlotte, breaking Will's heart... and Patrice's face (when Mark Donovan finds out and beats up the French Lothario).

Favourite quote: 'I'm single. I've been messing around with a few boys and now I'm looking for a real man.'

Fergus

Appearing in 'Home Alone', in the third series of the show, Fergus is the carrot-topped older gentlemen who whisks Will's mum away for the weekend after 'reconnecting' with her on Facebook, much to the amusement of the other Inbetweeners.

Mr Hopkins

Headmaster at Rudge Park Comprehensive and, although we only get a glimpse of him right back at the start of the show, he's clearly much nicer than his sadistic Head of Sixth Mr Gilbert!

There was a deleted scene with Hopkins in, where he welcomes Will to the new school, assuring him that he'll enjoy his time there: 'I think you'll find we're a happy school… this is a bully-free zone.' He couldn't have been more wrong though, as Will would end up having a photo of him taking a crap on his first day plastered around the school.

Jake

Another one of school bully Mark Donovan's goons, Jake is Mark's accomplice in taking pictures of Inbetweener Will in the school toilets on his first day.

James

This guy literally rolls onto our screens in *The Inbetweeners Movie*, when he runs into Simon with his quad bike. The club rep and party organiser plays the incident down as an accident but the eagle-eyed viewer will have spotted the snarl he gives Simon as he crashes into him while talking to Carli, who James has been dating during her holiday.

He becomes even more annoying as the film progresses, tricking Simon into handing over all of his clothes, threatening Jay in a club and insulting Jane at the boat party. Jay manages to pay him back for all of this though, when he's forced to give James a note so he can snort some cocaine. What James doesn't realise, however, is that he's been handed Jay's emergency fund, right from his arsehole. This leaves James trying to impress the girls with a piece of shit hanging off the end of his nose. Nice one, Jay!

Jane

The loudest of the girls the Inbetweeners meet on their lads' holiday to Malia, Jane appears right at the start of the film with the others on the coach, when Neil is on the lookout for 'chicas'.

Later that day when the groups cross paths again, Inbetweener Jay is less than complimentary about Jane because of her size but the pair end up sitting together at the bar while the other Inbetweeners perform the legendary dance in a terrible attempt to impress.

For some reason, Jane takes a liking to ignorant Inbetweener Jay, despite all of his bullshit tales and clear dislike of her. When the gang end up skinny dipping, the two almost have a moment but it's ruined by some idiots making fun of Jane's size and, with Jay too scared of being seen with her, it looks like the relationship is off before it ever gets going.

At the boat party though, towards the end of the film, Jay sees sense and, in a rare moment of maturity, tells Jane he wants to be seen with her. After a bit of fumbling around in the toilets, it's official and the pair look like an item, returning to the UK arm-in-arm. Poor Jane!

Favourite quote: 'Or what? I'll get harpooned because someone will mistake me for a whale? Someone will think they've discovered a new island? All the water will splash over onto the boat? I've heard them all. Take your pick.'

Joe

When the Inbetweeners take a trip to Warwick with Simon and Tara, we meet student Joe in the house he shares with Tara's sister, Sophie. Described by Sophie as 'a complete tool' because 'all he does is drink', and known to his drinking buddies as

Admiral, Joe lives up to the stereotype of living the typical life of a university student.

Will thinks that 'evenings at uni would consist of study, heated intellectual debate and avoiding elderly homosexual lecturers' but, through a number of drinking games, including one where Neil has to drink a load of orangeade mixed with fag butts, and plenty of weird sayings and chants, Joe shows Will that his ideas couldn't be further from the truth.

'Saucy Asda' Karen

Colleague and older love interest of Inbetweener Neil, Karen is never actually seen in the show but she does give the Inbetweener a scare. In 'Camping Trip', the final episode of the third series, Neil reveals to the others that Karen seduced him over the cheese counter at work and that now he's going to be a dad, after she texts him, writing, 'Did the test. It's positive. Thought you should know :/'

Luckily, this was just another time when Neil completely misunderstood something and Karen was actually telling him that she had tested positive for Chlamydia, not a child. Probably pretty fortunate, as Neil certainly isn't ready for fatherhood!

Paul Keenan

Paul is Will's ticket to get closer to Charlotte Hinchcliffe. When the pupil at Rudge Park Comprehensive gets smashed on a bottle of vodka before he's meant to take part in the fashion show alongside 'Big Jugs' Charlotte, Will – who had previously strongly objected to the whole idea of the show – snaps up the chance to take Paul's place.

THE INBETWEENERS

Mr Kennedy

Rudge Park Comp's rumoured paedophile, Kennedy appears in a couple of episodes in the series and seems to take a particular liking to Inbetweener Neil. The latter is oblivious to it all but Kennedy gets close on the Swanage field trip when he gets Neil to go swimming with him in a pair of Speedos in exchange for some vodka, and when he helps out in the dressing area at the school fashion show run by Carli D'Amato.

Kerry

Things are looking up for Will in the third series of the show when he's invited on a blind date with Kerry, who's given her last three boyfriends a blow-job. The only problem is that things are literally 'looking up', as lofty Kerry towers over the much shorter Will.

After weighing up his options, and after a few kisses, Will decides that the best thing to do is end the relationship, which he does badly, leaving Kerry in tears. She ends up giving Neil a couple of birthday blow-jobs later that night, much to virgin Will's annoyance.

Dinner lady

When the Inbetweeners head off to Malia for their first lads' holiday, Neil is certain he isn't going to cheat on his beloved Nicole. But less than 24 hours in, after showing some of his best dance moves, he can be seen in the middle of the dance floor at Marco's 'finger-banging' a dinner lady who's at least 20 years his senior. He ends up taking her back to the hotel for some more 'romance', where Will likens her to Johnny Vegas.

Afterwards, Neil insists he was faithful to his girlfriend back home: 'We weren't kissing and only the tip went in. Any more than the tip is cheating and I'd never do that 'cause I've got ethics,' but we're not too sure! We last see the dinner lady waddling away from the lads' hotel and pulling her undies out of her arse crack.

Samantha Leah

Despite his tales of wild sex and orgies, it's not often that Inbetweener Jay gets lucky with the ladies. But during the school Christmas party at the end of the first series, Jay looks to have met his match with Samantha when he's getting ready to get on the decks, as she tells him, 'I used to deejay at a top club in Ibiza. I could probably get you a spot. You look like you're really into it.'

We find out later that she even gave Jay an 'over-the-trousers wank' behind the decks, although he did try to make out it was a 'blowy' at first. Typical Jay!

Favourite quote: 'Are you bent?'

Lewis

Lewis is another one of the students we meet when the lads take a trip to Warwick. Like his housemates, he loves drink, drink and more drink. A typical student really.

Lisa

Part of the group of girls the lads meet in Malia in *The Inbetweeners Movie*, Lisa stands out as the 'Neil' of her group and, not surprisingly, her and Neil hit it off quickly when they meet in Malia's not-so-hot spot, Marco's Club.

Conversation between the pair is nil but, when Neil asks her for a dance, she jumps at the chance and quickly starts mimicking some of his signature moves. Neil looks like he's blown it though, when he leaves Lisa to start dancing with a pair of very mature women.

Lucy

Part of the foursome the lads meet in Marco's Club in *The Inbetweeners Movie*, Lucy looks like she might just be the girl to finally take Simon's mind off ex-Carli D'Amato but, even after making the first move to introduce herself and getting a really awkward reply ('Hi, I'm Dimon. SIMON, I'm Simon') conversation quickly moves to Carli and Lucy's interest is obviously lost. She still decides, however, to invite the guys to an all-day boat party later that week.

Mr McKenzie

Played by Nescafé ad man Anthony Head, Will's dad is mentioned throughout the series but doesn't make his first on-screen appearance until the first film.

It's because of Mr McKenzie's wandering eyes that Will and his mum Polly move house when he turfs them out for the babysitter, Susie. And when we finally meet Will's dad, it's clear that he's still only really interested in the younger Susie, breaking the news that the pair are now married and didn't bother inviting Will because it was just close family and friends!

Polly McKenzie

When Will McKenzie starts his first term at Rudge Park Comprehensive, he doesn't make the greatest of impressions but his mum, on the other hand, does!

Polly likes to think she's got Will's safety as her top priority so, without thinking about the embarrassment factor for her son, she decides it's best to pick him up and drop him off right outside the school gates. This, however, gives Will's friends (Neil, Jay and Simon) and his enemies (Mark Donovan) the perfect chance to gawp at the attractive Mrs McKenzie.

It starts with, 'Is that your mum?' from Simon and quickly descends into filth with Jay saying, 'I'd fuck her… Look, all I wanna know is whether you'd get down between her knees, spread them and…'

Some of our other favourite Polly-related quotes are Jay's: 'Have you ever had a wank over Will's mum?', 'Wanking over your mum's bra', 'Well, I didn't hear your mum complaining… although her mouth was full at the time' and favourite of all, by French exchange-student Patrice: 'Uh, I just had a really nice tug thinking about your mother. And I think some went on the floor, sorry.'

It's pretty obvious that Polly likes the attention and she's very friendly with all of the boys, especially Patrice, who she has a bit of a moment with when they lock eyes.

We don't find out too much about Polly's love life, other than in the third series when she leaves Will home alone for the weekend to meet up with 'an old friend', and that Will's dad left her for a younger woman.

Will McKenzie

Considered by many as the star of the show, and definitely our favourite Inbetweener, it's thanks to 'briefcase wanker' Will (and his dad's wondering eye) that the awesome foursome exists!

When his parents divorce and Will is forced to attend a public comprehensive, it doesn't look like he's going to enjoy his life in the sixth form but, thanks to Simon, Jay and Neil, the socially dysfunctional teenager has a decent laugh (most of the time).

Despite his MANY flaws, including his ability to insult at the drop of a hat (think Big Kerry, Thorpe Park, Alison…), the fact that he shit himself in an exam, his dreadful fashion sense and terrible luck with the ladies, Will is a pretty nice guy.

Favourite quotes:

'Can we please stop talking about my mother's VAGINA?!'

'First stop the Minoan Palace in Knossos.'

'Yes but it's our shithole! So I say we get out there and get royally fucked up on Jay's dead granddad's money!'

'You need to see a bowel specialist!'

'But they do say whatever doesn't kill you makes you stronger. Except polio.'

'Yes, I'll suspend my sympathy as I'm covered in your piss!'

'They had a gang based on masturbation? Oh, there's nothing gay about that.'

'Has she got any special dietary requirements? It's just I've never cooked for an imaginary woman before.'

'I thought it was a fart, sir, I thought it was safe.'

'It's not fucking true! People don't get fingered for a bet, Jay. With the possible exception of your sister.'

Danny Moore

Danny, the 12-year-old hard man from Rudge Park Comp, appears in the second episode of the second series, 'Work Experience'. Living on the notorious Northwood estate, Danny proves that size isn't everything after bumping into Simon in the corridor at school and threatening to 'do-in' the much older Inbetweener after being called a 'short-arse'.

His threats are wrongly brushed off by Si and, later in the episode, while Simon is mid-wank with Hannah Fields from the year below, Danny runs over, pushes Simon over and kicks him numerous times, denting Simon's chance of love, his pride and, worst of all, his cock. Ouch! He then groups together his Northwood gang, leaving Si and the other Inbetweeners quivering in the toilets.

Angry neighbour

Anyone would be pissed off if they caught four idiots vandalising their garden and Will's neighbour isn't any different. In the fifth episode of the final series, when the lads are given free reign at Will's place after his mum heads off for a saucy weekend away, they kill a bit of time by kicking and swinging gold clubs at flowers in this fella's garden. He eventually catches up with them and, in a red-faced outrage, screams at the petrified lads through Will's front-room window. Luckily for them, the angry man is subdued by the good looks of Will's mum, who gets back just in time.

Nicole

The fish counter at the local supermarket is where some of the greatest romances have played out and it's while working there in *The Inbetweeners Movie* that Neil meets girlfriend Nicole. When Neil leaves for his lads' holiday in Malia, he vows to be faithful to Nicole, but she gets a bit of a shock at the end of the movie when he returns home with Lisa and runs off through the terminal.

Nicos

Appearing in the first film, Nicos is the Greek bartender boyfriend of the gorgeous Alison, who catches Will's attention from the start. Luckily for the Inbetweener, Nicos is a bit of a tit and is caught by the pair having sex on the beach (not the cocktail) with another English tourist. After being a bit of a tit himself, this eventually leaves the door open for Will to swoop in.

Patrice

Chain-smoking, smouldering-eyed Patrice is the French exchange student who stays over at Inbetweener Simon's for a week as part of a school programme. The lads try to ignore Patrice as much as possible, probably because they realise he's much cooler than them.

This shows when Patrice is the only one out of the gang allowed into a house party, where he ends up sleeping with Charlotte Hinchcliffe, much to Will's annoyance! He's also got a couple of older fans too, with Will's and Simon's mums both taking a bit of a shine to the good-looking French kid.

Rachel

Rachel is best mates with Carli D'Amato and appears in the three series and the first film. She's less than impressed by the Inbetweeners, especially Simon, and can often be seen sighing or rolling her eyes at Simon's geeky, awkward comments.

She also has a run-in with Will when the lads follow Rachel and Carli on a night out to London. Will does his best to impress her, treating the outing like a date with Rachel from the off, but she quickly passes up her 'golden' opportunity with the Inbetweener, opting for another guy, Dean.

Richard

At it on his own, 'having a mental time', Richard is a loner the gang meet when they first arrive in Malia in *The Inbetweeners Movie*. Not only does he try and bum a beer off the lads but he then goes on to ask for a shower at their apartment! He's definitely one of the odder characters we meet in the film.

We last see him at the boat party, where he explains to Neil that he couldn't stop crying so his mum and dad have flown over to collect him (and they're at the boat party). This is their only mention in this list. With a son like Richard, they don't deserve any more!

Mr Sethi

According to Simon's dad, if you need a suit, old Mr Sethi is the man to see. It was at his shop where Si's dad hired the suit he wore when he first slept with his mum, with Mr Sethi going mad because it was returned covered in grass stains.

He's very kind to his customers when they're trying on his 'classic' suits, often made of suede, velvet and complemented with ruffles and satin. Nice!

Favourite quote: 'Too jazzy?'

Alistair Scott

Alistair appears in the first episode of series three when he returns to the lads' school to watch a charity fashion show organised in his honour, after recovering from kidney failure.

The pupils of Rudge Park rally round Alistair (even though he is a bit of a knob) but the Inbetweeners see through this and Jay, in particular, takes a strong disliking to the kid: 'I never liked him when he was well, I never liked him when he was ill and I don't like him now he's getting better. Simples.'

This is probably one of the few occasions where Jay's weird logic actually makes sense and, of course, the event doesn't go smoothly and ends with the entire audience seeing Inbetweener Simon's bollock!

Susie

Fellow new-starter at Rudge Park Comprehensive, Susie appears in two episodes of the series. On their first day, even Will tries to avoid Susie, who is taking her A Levels four years early for her 'geekiness'.

She does get close to one of the Inbetweeners though, when lofty Neil wins an unwanted date with her and ends up (along with Susie's mum) sharing a bargain bucket at the local KFC!

Step-mum Susie

The reason for Will's parents' break-up, Susie is mentioned right back in series one of the show as the babysitter his dad ran off with but it's not until the first film that we see her. Attractive, and much younger than Will's dad, we get the impression that Susie doesn't take her role as stepmother too seriously, as she seems to almost ignore the Inbetweener completely, not even inviting him to her wedding to his father.

Sophie

Another girl who doesn't warm to the Inbetweeners, Sophie is the sister of Simon's short-term girlfriend Tara. When Simon and Tara decide to take their relationship to the next level, they realise they need to go somewhere where they can have a bit of privacy away from their annoying parents.

So it's off to Sophie's student house in Warwick, where they're told they can share a room. Sophie isn't too impressed that the pair are having sex but at least they're not doing it in the bushes at the back of the garden (Simon's suggestion).

It's not too much of a surprise that she doesn't like Simon when, after telling the pair that she's 'not mad keen on the idea of you two having sex at all but at least I know you're doing it somewhere comfortable,' Si replies, 'Oh, absolutely. Only in her vagina.' Hardly the greatest first impression ever made!

But after showing her sister where the condoms and spare sheets are (oh, the romance), she leaves them to it. That is until she hears her little sister screaming because Si's started punching his cock, and she throws the boys out of the house!

Katie Sutherland

Not all of the Sutherlands are awkward and lofty like Inbetweener Neil. In fact, his elder sister Katie is quite the opposite. Of course, the other Inbetweeners love the fact that Neil's sister is stunning and try their best to chat to her. Obviously, she's aware of this and does her best to ignore the boys.

Kevin Sutherland

Softly spoken Kevin (Neil's dad) appears in several episodes of the show and also in the first film. Neil takes a lot of stick from the other Inbetweeners about his dad. First, because they don't have much money and, second, they all reckon he's gay.

This leads to several awkward moments in the show, including the time Will calls him a massive 'bumder' after skipping school and getting drunk, and when Pam Cooper (Si's mum) openly refers to him as gay while defending him against being called a paedophile.

Neil Sutherland

The slowest of the group, Inbetweener Neil is a bit of an odd one. He seems to be the only one of the lads who does his own thing without ever mentioning it to anyone. This includes working at Thorpe Park, learning to drive and numerous sexual encounters.

In fact, Neil actually does quite well with the ladies. Throughout the series he gets with a number of girls, including the goth at Caravan Club, Big Kerry and numerous more mature women in Malia.

This is probably because, unlike the others, Neil doesn't take himself too seriously. Revealing in the first film that 'I stopped believing in God when I realised it was just dog spelled backwards', he happily plods along with life and takes what's thrown at him in his stride (if he even realises what's going on half the time).

Favourite quotes:

'Yeah, you sit on your arm till your hand goes dead. Ten, fifteen minutes is normally enough. And then, when you wank, it feels like someone else is doing it.'

'How much Lego can you get up your bum? Didn't you do it as a kid? Just a triangle one and a long one? Maybe a few singles?'

'I wasn't wanking! My cock is cut... my cock is cut!'

'Not sure, mate, could be fart, could be worse... Calm down, it was only a Sausage and Egg McMuffin. Oh, There's the hash brown!'

Tara Brown

Every now and again, Inbetweener Simon seems to get a little bit of interest from the opposite sex and it's in the second episode of the third series, 'The Gig and the Girlfriend', when Simon meets Tara.

After being rejected by Carli (again), Simon gets chatting to Tara, who tells him about a gig that's coming up. Obviously out to impress, he lets on that he's planning on going to it too and somehow ends up promising to score some weed for them.

After a comedy of errors that includes Jay buying tea instead of weed, Will getting stoned and Tara throwing up, the pair end up kissing and are an item by the next episode.

Things are looking good for the two and Tara even tries to set Will up with her mate 'Big Kerry' but, after an epic failure during a trip to Warwick where the two plan to have sex for the first time, Tara texts Simon telling him to NEVER get in touch again.

The master tattooist

So you're probably thinking, 'I don't remember this one.' Don't worry, you're not going mad. The master tattooist is a character from the first film played by 1980s singer Christos Tolera, who performed as part of the band Blue Rondo à la Turk. He only filmed one scene of the movie, which was used in some of the promo clips before it opened but the sequence never made the final cut.

In the deleted scene, Jay and Neil, like many drunk Brits abroad, have decided to go to get a tattoo but the master tattooist doesn't quite live up to his name and, thanks to confusion over a J and a G, Neil ends up with 'Gay Neil Malia' on his shoulder.

We'd love to have seen Kevin's face when he returned to the UK with that one!

The tramp

When Simon gets knocked back from a London nightclub for wearing a pair of trainers, he decides to do the obvious and swap his brand-new kicks for a pair of tramp's shoes. Unfortunately for Simon, the Scottish tramp had pissed in them first, ruining his chances yet again with his beloved Carli.

Tom

Described by Simon as 'a lanky twat', Tom appears in the very first episode of the show as the new boyfriend of Carli D'Amato. Much to Si's annoyance, Tom is taller, older and has a driving licence. His relationship with Carli is on and off because he's a bit more interested in seeing his rugby mates, and in the 'Xmas Party' episode in series two the couple split before later getting back together.

Miss Timms

The 'TILF' of Rudge Park Comp, Miss Timms, appears in the last episode of the first series at the Christmas party organised by Will. Neil reveals his soft spot for Timms early on in the episode: 'It should be illegal for her to teach biology. I almost knocked one out there and then when we did the reproduction system.'

And after going all out and getting an Elvis-style flared suit with a low-cut front, he makes his move at the party. The shocked Timms pulls away quicker than Big John at a buffet but it's too late for Neil as the whole of the sixth form has seen him being turned down, with rumours that she and Head of Sixth, Mr Gilbert, are romantically involved.

John Webster, aka Big John

John is a fellow new-starter at Rudge Park Comprehensive with Inbetweener Will in the first ever episode of the show. Actor John Seaward impressed so much at auditions that *The Inbetweeners* writers Damon Beesley and Iain Morris wrote a role specifically for him to play!

Big John by name and nature gets a pretty tough time at Rudge Park and receives a fair amount of stick from his fellow pupils, including the Inbetweeners. He does have some happy times though, most notably touching a boob at a house party and organising the catering for the Rudge Park Comp Xmas prom.

Favourite quote: 'Lasagna's nice and so are burgers. You don't need a plate for burgers, which gives them an edge on lasagna.'

Wolfie

When Will's work-experience plans of starting out his career in journalism are mixed up with Neil's, he finds himself with a placement in a garage alongside 17-year-old mechanic Wolfie in the second episode of the second series. Looking more like a dad than a kid, Wolfie doesn't take much of a liking to Will, who's pretty rude about his profession, so decides to get his own back by sending him on wild errands, throwing him in a lake and ruining his chances (again) with Charlotte Hinchcliffe by revealing everything Will had said about her 'big titties'.

CHAPTER NINE

THE FUTURE

Before *The Inbetweeners Movie 2* was scheduled to start filming there were several other projects for the original stars to get their teeth into. Here are a few highlights of what's been going on and a sneak-peak of what could be in the pipeline after the long-awaited *Inbetweeners Movie* sequel.

Simon Bird

Since playing Will McKenzie in *The Inbetweeners*, Simon Bird has prided himself on playing characters that bear a similar resemblance to him in real life: 'All the people I love are being themselves, like Larry David.' This is particularly noticeable in his satirical acting style in many of the roles he has played since the hit TV show, such as in *Chickens* and *Friday Night Dinner*, where there are a good few instances of his character being the butt of the joke, finding awkward situations but still possessing quick wit and charm in a timely but sarcastic manner. Don't expect him to play a psychotic, crazed killer or the new Jason Bourne anytime soon!

Chickens, the sitcom written by Simon Bird, Joe Thomas and Jonny Sweet, was scheduled for a six-part first series in 2013 by Sky 1 and enjoyed modest reviews consistent with those of the first series of *The Inbetweeners*. However, it is yet to be confirmed whether there will be a subsequent second series in 2014.

The critically acclaimed *Friday Night Dinner*, in which Bird co-starred with Tamsin Greig, Paul Ritter, Tom Rosenthal and Mark Heap, was commissioned for a third series last year and aired in the early months of 2014. It is yet to be seen whether Channel 4 will commission a fourth series of the sitcom.

There's no doubt that Simon Bird's future lies within comedy. However, if it were up to his parents, they would much rather he finished his PhD in Philosophy! In an interview with the *Radio Times*, Bird plays down his success and says he feels he still has to prove to certain people that his chosen career path was the right move. 'None of my and Joe's [Thomas] acclaim or fame has come from anything we've created ourselves. I guess I feel that I have stuff to prove.' It's pretty clear that the path he has taken means there will be more comedy writing coming up for Simon. At the beginning of his career, he is candid about wanting to be a comedian rather than an actor, so writing seems to be the medium that he feels most comfortable with.

Joe Thomas

Similarly to Simon Bird, Joe Thomas has adopted his own style, which he doesn't plan on changing any time soon. 'My heroes were always writers. [When starting out] I wanted to be Ricky Gervais or Stephen Merchant.' Coming from the same educational background as Simon Bird, Joe Thomas also has aspirations to be a comedy writer and co-writing and starring in *Chickens* seems to be the start of that process.

In the Sky 1 series *Chickens*, Joe Thomas plays the character of George Wright, who bears an uncanny resemblance to his *Inbetweeners* character Simon Cooper when it comes to his lacklustre attempts to woo the ladies. As with Simon Bird, Joe is very much an advocate of playing characters who are recognisable to himself, hence the admiration for Gervais and Merchant.

The most well-known TV series that Joe Thomas has starred in post-*Inbetweeners* is the Channel 4 comedy *Fresh Meat*, a show about a group of students living together in a house in Manchester, which also starred stand-up comedian Jack Whitehall. The series has been a great success and has already run for three seasons from 2011–2013. At the time of the end of the third series in December 2013, Sam Bain, one of the many co-writers of *Fresh Meat*, has already hinted that they are planning to write a fourth series and even implied that there could be a film adaptation in the pipeline – an idea that was sparked after the massive success of *The Inbetweeners Movie* in 2011.

James Buckley

The future for James Buckley couldn't be more different to the one you may have expected for his character Jay Cartwright in *The Inbetweeners*. The actor is now fully settled down with wife Claire Meek and has two young children to look after, a million miles away from what you'd expect from his immature and crude alter-ego Jay, who would probably still be telling far-fetched tales of debauchery and promiscuity by now!

In terms of his career, James has taken very much a broad creative view of his work going forwards and 2014 should see him not only stretch his acting talents but also his forte and passion for music. Buckley is very much a music connoisseur and, since *The Inbetweeners*, he has performed with Steve Craddock (of Brit-pop band Ocean Colour Scene) and directed and featured in the music videos of many up-and-coming UK bands.

As well as his music, we should expect more voiceover activity from James too; his distinct voice has been noticeable on a number of advertisements over the past year, mostly for brands that require a playful and cheeky voice as their 'ambassador'.

Undoubtedly, James Buckley is the biggest *Inbetweeners* star on Twitter. His sneak-peaks about *The Inbetweeners Movie 2* while on location in Australia have given the fans lots to talk about in the lead-up to the new film. And with over 200,000 followers, expect many more tweets and banter about all things *Inbetweeners*, babies and Crystal Palace!

Blake Harrison

Since appearing as halfwit Neil Sutherland in *The Inbetweeners*, Blake has appeared in a number of short films and has made small appearances as one-off characters in TV series, most notably as Barney in *Him & Her*, which concluded in December 2014.

Blake's most notable roles came in 2013, when he played Ben and Scott in respective sitcoms *Big Bad World* and *Way to Go*. The Comedy Central sitcom *Big Bad World* sees Blake play a hapless student who returns from university without a job or a girlfriend. The show received modest reviews and rumours are circulating about a potential second series to be aired sometime in 2014.

In a recent interview with the *Daily Mail*, Blake revealed that he would love to play a superhero: 'I'm a big comic-book geek so playing a superhero would be huge. As a skinny guy, the ideal superhero would be Spider-Man, but Andrew Garfield is doing a pretty good job, so it might have to be The Flash.'

We think Blake has got some way to go before playing his favourite superhero but his army of over 100,000 Twitter followers may disagree! Throughout the filming of the new *Inbetweeners* film, Blake gave us many insights into life 'down-under' and even a few sneaks at some stills from the film.

Greg Davies

The one and only Mr Gilbert has gone on to produce a couple of highly acclaimed stand-up shows following *The Inbetweeners*. Both *Firing Cheeseballs at a Dog* in 2011 and *The Back of My Mum's Head* in 2013 were well received by the critics and, no doubt, we will see more stand-up from Greg in 2014 and beyond.

Probably the biggest appearance since Mr Gilbert, was playing Ken Thompson in the BBC3 sitcom *Cuckoo*. At the time, *Cuckoo* was the channel's most-watched comedy launch and *Digital Spy* has reported that a second series should be due for transmission in 2014. In addition, in 2013 Davies wrote and starred in the Channel 4 sitcom *Man Down*. The first series was well received and Greg announced a second series during his stand-up tour.

Whatever happens for Greg Davies, one thing is for sure: he'll remain 'big' for the foreseeable future. When asked about the size of his career and his height, the 6ft, 8in star told *bigissue.com*, 'I still feel like a ludicrously tall, fat man.'

CHAPTER TEN

FAREWELL

If the rumours are true and the film this summer is to be the last we see of *The Inbetweeners*, we'll be sad to see them go but happy that they've given us so many memories and broadened our vocabulary over the past six years! There aren't many British comedies that have inspired a generation, made us laugh out loud and introduced us to a new raft of words we'll surely never forget! How many of us now use the phrase 'fwiend' when speaking about somebody outside of our immediate group of acquaintances? And how many times have you made that annoying noise 'beep de beep beep' when a mate is talking about their latest girlfriend? However, if there's one word we can use that captivates this amazing show, 'clunge' has to be it. Goodbye, bumders!